I HATE PEOPLE!

Also by Jonathan Littman

The Ten Faces of Innovation:
IDEO's Strategies for Beating
the Devil's Advocate & Driving Creativity
throughout Your Organization *(with Tom Kelley)*

We Shall Not Fail:
The Inspiring Leadership of Winston Churchill
(with Celia Sandys)

The Art of Innovation:
Lessons in Creativity from IDEO,
America's Leading Design Firm *(with Tom Kelley)*

The Beautiful Game:
Sixteen Girls and the Soccer Season
That Changed Everything

The Fugitive Game:
Online with Kevin Mitnick

Watchman:
The Twisted Life and Crimes
of Serial Hacker Kevin Poulsen

Once Upon a Time in ComputerLand:
The Amazing, Billion-Dollar Tale of Bill Millard

I HATE PEOPLE!

*Kick Loose from the Overbearing and
Underhanded Jerks at Work and
Get What You Want Out of Your Job*

JONATHAN LITTMAN
MARC HERSHON

Little, Brown and Company   New York   Boston   London

Little, Brown and Company
Hachette Book Group
237 Park Avenue, New York, NY 10017
Visit our Web site at www.HachetteBookGroup.com

First Edition: June 2009

Little, Brown and Company is a division of Hachette Book Group, Inc. The Little, Brown name and logo are trademarks of Hachette Book Group, Inc.

Illustrations by Bill Murray

Library of Congress Cataloging-in-Publication Data
Littman, Jonathan.
  I hate people! : kick loose from the overbearing and underhanded jerks at work and get what you want out of your job / Jonathan Littman, Marc Hershon. – 1st ed.
      p. cm.
  ISBN 978-0-316-03229-2/978-0-316-06882-6 (int'l ed.)
  1. Quality of work life.   2. Interpersonal conflict.   3. Interpersonal relations.   I. Hershon, Marc.   II. Title.
  HD6955.H39 2009
  650.1'3 – dc22   2008051575

10 9 8 7 6 5 4 3 2 1

RRD-IN

Book design by Meryl Sussman Levavi

Printed in the United States of America

For Debra
– M.H.

For Elizabeth, Kate, and Sherry
– J.L.

Contents

I HATE PEOPLE!

1. I Hate People

I hate people.

Where'd we get that idea? We listened. We heard people muttering "I hate people" whenever things would get stressful. Like, every single day. This is not a new problem, and the evidence suggests it's getting worse by the second, thanks to remarkable advances in technology that have had the unintended effect of making it far easier for people to annoy us. The billions of e-mails, v-mails, and text messages sent every day threaten to overwhelm us like a plague of e-locusts.

We hate people who play favorites, people who make the rules, people who don't give others a break. You know who we're talking about. The people who lie in the shadows of your meeting, and after you've just made an awesome presentation, stab you with, "Excuse me, but have our customers asked for this?"

Part of the problem stems from a lack of trust. More than seven out of ten Americans distrust the CEOs of large corporations. Only a third of employees believe that "senior management communicates openly and honestly," according to a recent survey by Towers Perrin of ninety thousand workers in eighteen countries; two-thirds believe their bosses can't or won't talk straight. Survey after survey has shown that half of the workforce does not trust its superiors. Recent McKinsey research has revealed that fundamental values of honesty and candor are missing in a growing percentage of companies.

The numbers suggest a crisis – one not likely to be solved by organizations or corporations anytime soon. Consider that the federal government's Bureau of Labor Statistics does not even track worker satisfaction.

People are what bring us down, make us scream obscenities in our cars, mutter things under our breath in our cubicles, and shout in the elevator when we're alone.

The Perfect Holiday

What were one-third of fifteen hundred British workers willing to do?
Forgo a week's holiday if they didn't have to work next to people they hated.

Denial has been widespread, but we don't believe it's possible to keep a lid on the truth. People are angry – and today, they're a lot less likely to keep quiet about it.

On Facebook, the popular online social network, users

have generated an "Enemybook" option, where People Haters can air their feuds. In mid-2008, the *New York Times* ran a front-page story about another kind of broken relationship getting headlines. An astonishing number of ex-spouses are furiously trashing their former beloveds on popular blogs on the Internet. The courts are doing little to stem the vilifying, and as the *Times* reported, "The confessions can stretch toward eternity in a steady stream of enraged or despondent postings."

The constraints of the workplace and fear of lawsuits have bottled up similar fury against irritating cubemates and meddling bosses. But despite these roadblocks, we had no trouble finding dozens of blogs and websites that play to our basic frustration at the office – sites with names like Anger Central, Disgruntled Workforce, and Team Building Is for Suckers.

These feelings are not a joke. Consider what a former lieutenant commander in the navy told us of his experience working on Wall Street as an investment banker: "I was an unmitigated failure. I had no idea how to navigate through these difficult people. One Sunday after Thanksgiving of 2004, I was homicidal. I was going to kill my boss. I was fighting to swim and he had his arms around my neck, strangling me." What makes this story even more striking is that the lieutenant commander prided himself on being a solid leader of 120 men in the military, dedicating himself to his missions in Kosovo, Guam, and Estonia.

Burnout is the common affliction of driven, obsessive professionals. "In 21st-century New York, the 60-hour week is considered normal," writes *New York* magazine. "In some professions, it's a status symbol. But burnout, for the most part, is considered a sign of weakness, a career killer." Workers don't burn out just because they work too hard. Workers burn out because of *people*. A classic 1990s management study showed that workers who have frequent intense or emotionally charged interactions with other people are more susceptible to what's referred to as emotional exhaustion.

The past few years many Americans have discovered that a lack of accountability got our country, economy, and institutions into a whole lot of trouble. Regulators were too nice to hedge funds and speculators and Wall Street. Bernie Madoff allegedly ripped off individuals and companies to the tune of $50 billion – by pretending to be nice. This isn't the first time this has happened in American business. The Crash of '29 was another case where people weren't willing to ask the tough questions. While the first years of the new millennium were defined by this fixation on superficial niceness, we believe we're entering a new era. Practical People Hating directed toward those demanding our enmity – bankers, Fed chairmen, politicians, and other miscreants who have mucked up our 401ks and fractured our financial infrastructure. A democratic society, built on free trade, has no room for those willing to rig the game and harm millions of people. There are serious consequences for not People Hating enough. Our nation has discovered, in the past decade, how a minority of bad apples can rot not just the rest of the fruit but the barrel as well. The time has come to face reality.

Studies and countless real-life stories clearly demonstrate that people are hating people. Yes, at your very own office. We work too many hours, meet too often, travel too much, and e-mail constantly. Burnout or cowering in your cubicle or office are not viable options.

The Rude Game

89 percent of people say rudeness is a serious problem.

78 percent say it's gotten worse in the past ten years.

99 percent of people say they aren't rude.

— *U.S. News & World Report*

For those readers wondering whether we're serious, a brief note of explanation. We like and sometimes even love individuals. It's people we hate. Many of you may genuinely enjoy the company of your office mates. There's a reason for that. These are people who fall within the standards and expectations you set for your daily interactions. The men and women whose natural shortcomings are offset by their capabilities and character. The problem with most people is that they rarely bother to belly up to this relationship point. They just stand in your way, annoy, and irritate. At times, facing them can be more than we can stand. As comedian Rich Hall said in Seattle back in the 1980s when he was found hiding in the kitchen of the Comedy Underground after his show one night, "I like people. Just not in a group."

This book is designed for businesspeople who recognize the difference between genuine individuals and people. Men and women who know they can't wait for some promised corporate utopia. Being nice when everyone else is just *playing* nice is not wise. Nor is it good for your career. Now that you've gotten this far, we should let you know what you're getting into. You're about to undertake a Discipline. Like karate or judo. Think of it as jujitsu for outsmarting the corporate oafs.

Who are these oafs? We call them the Ten Least Wanted. Many other books have focused on the positive people in business. Happy people. Creative people. Productive people. The Ten Least Wanted are just the opposite. They are the Stop Signs, the naysayers who block your every idea. The Switchblades, those underhanded jerks who take credit for your work. That Flimflam down the hall with a snarky tendency to trick you into doing his work for him. Then there's Minute Man, who steals your time in bite-size chunks that eat up your day. This is just a glimpse of a few of the men and women who keep us from doing our work and realizing our dreams. We'll be meeting them and the rest of the Ten Least Wanted in depth in the chapters to come, learning skills and strategies for defeating them.

It's time to take action. In your hands you hold the key to keeping people out of your face.

Everyone hates people at some point. And if you say you don't, you're lying.

Don't worry: it's not a bad thing. The contributions of People Haters are increasingly respected and even sought out. Brad Bird, the director of *The Incredibles* and *Ratatouille,* two of Pixar's crop of amazing computer-generated films, chooses to work with computer artists who are People Haters: employees who have become frustrated because their individual approaches to the medium are not valued by the industry at large. Bird called them "black sheep" in an interview in the *McKinsey Quarterly.* When he was tackling the animation job on *The Incredibles,* he sought out these malcontents, believing they held the keys to novel ways of working faster, more creatively, even less expensively. "We gave the black sheep a chance to prove their theories," said Bird, "and we changed the way a number of things are done here."

"I hate mankind, for I think of myself as one of the best of them, and I know how bad I am."
— SAMUEL JOHNSON

We believe that all of us can get smarter about dealing with people at work. Companies think nothing of devoting major resources to a competitive market analysis for a new product introduction. They assume competitors will try to knock off their innovation. Undercut their pricing. Steal their design. That's business. Well, the evidence is in and it's clear these same forces apply on a human level. Coworkers, partners, and bosses – they don't always have your best interests at heart.

Just as you don't assume competitors love you, it's naive to think everyone you work with thinks you're terrific. The only person you can trust to have your back in this crazy business world is yourself. But today, who has the time or, more important, guts to be themselves? If you're constantly e-mailing, texting, and calling, chances are you've developed a pile of masks and personae to deal with others.

These electronic facades are not your best selves. You might even hate them a bit. Once you face that truth, you can begin to be your true self. And let's face it, there are a lot of people in your company that your true self would rather not call, e-mail, or text.

Yes, we understand that our path isn't the politically correct approach to resolving business conflict. We know those books and articles by well-meaning authors: *How to Be Your Coworker's Best Buddy. Seven Steps to Becoming the Office Pushover. Happy Work: A Practical Guide. It's Me, Not You. How to Stop Making Your Boss a Bully. You're the Reason Your Office Is Miserable. Help Me Stop Hurting You. I'm a Hungry Little Mouse.*

These works share a common thread: You're to blame. Nobody else. It all goes back to your childhood, your education, your home life. You.

That boss driving you nuts? You just don't understand him. That coworker stealing credit for your great ideas? You should have spoken up sooner.

What's missing here? Honesty.

We know what you're saying: "I don't hate people. I like people."

Of course you do. That's how you were brought up. That's the "right" attitude. You open doors for old ladies. Let strangers cut in line. Don't mind when people butt in on your conversations. Of course you don't hate people.

Here's your chance to prove it. Take the following test and see just how much people make your day.

The *I Hate People!* Quiz

A. When I'm on a business flight I most enjoy sitting beside . . .

1. chatty, large people wearing lots of cologne.
2. crying children.
3. children.
4. an empty seat.
5. two empty seats.

B. During a company meeting I most enjoy . . .

1. watching a long, dry PowerPoint presentation.
2. people repeating themselves. Again.
3. people texting constantly.
4. frequent breaks.
5. leaving.

C. I love it when my coworker . . .

1. watches YouTube videos on his PC.
2. eats stinky food at his desk.
3. clips his nails.
4. calls in sick.
5. quits.

D. I like my boss most when he . . .

1. e-mails me every half hour.
2. peers over my shoulder.
3. jokes about firing me.
4. is delayed flying home.
5. is on vacation.

E. My favorite office noise is somebody . . .

1. clearing his throat.
2. slurping his coffee.
3. tapping his pencil.
4. squeaking his desk chair.
5. snapping his gum.

F. I love overhearing workplace conversation about . . .

1. the boyfriend.
2. the girlfriend.
3. the spouse.
4. the kids.
5. how much someone hates his job.

G. The office food I like most is . . .

1. vending-machine sandwiches.
2. onion bagels.
3. cardboard pizza.
4. Tupperware Surprise.
5. hand-fouled candy from an open dish.

Congratulations! You've just completed a psychological self-exploration that will grant you fresh insights into your level of People Hating. Total up your score and check it against the following scale.

1–7 You really *do* like people. Consider seeking professional help.

8–13 There's hope: you're not a total glutton for punishment.

14–21 Clearly, you're on the path to realizing people aren't all they're cracked up to be.

22–29 You are a People Hater. Though you've got natural talent, you could use some additional skills.

30–35 Devout People Hater. Welcome, friend! Get ready to turn your natural skills into business assets.

THE PATH OF THE SOLOIST

We admire those of you independent and strong enough to rise above your cubicles and dare to be productive People Haters. You deserve a term of your own. We offer the Soloist. Bold enough to create the attitude, space, and time to stretch your career and expand your life. Ready to take that critical step toward becoming one of those happy souls who deftly works alone or collaborates with just a handful of other talented people . . . while artfully deflecting all the rest. Because while you can't change the people you hate, you *can* stop them from dragging you down.

You'll discover that you're learning a counterintuitive approach to coping with problem people. We're bringing the power of redirecting and avoiding the emotional blows dished out by bosses, coworkers, and competitors. While you may need a lot of these people to get through your day, your career, and your life . . . nobody said you have to like them.

The first step along the Path of the Soloist is to be able to identify the Ten Least Wanted. These are the people in the office who pose the greatest threat to your ability to get your work done. They're coworkers, managers, bosses, and clients. We've classified these ten archetypes under three categories: Stumbling Blocks, Wrong Turns, and Time Wasters. In the first part of the book, you'll learn to identify and defuse the power of the Ten Least Wanted to screw up your day.

I Hate People! will help you learn:

- ▶ **How to** form Ensembles with other Soloists — the best kind of teamwork.
- ▶ **How to** Solocraft, a way of working that increases your effectiveness and productivity, both alone and in a group.
- ▶ **How to** skip or cut short unnecessary meetings, conference calls, and other forms of corporate drudgery to increase your solo time.
- ▶ **How to** minimize and even eliminate progress-stifling interruptions throughout your day.
- ▶ **How to** push things off your plate to help you stay on track while juggling multiple projects.

- ► **How to** dig your Cave, creating the ideal space in which to get away and get your work done.
- ► **How to** Island Hop, creating the little refreshing breaks in your workday that give you a chance to relax while leading you to creative breakthroughs.

Ready to get started?
Go ahead.
Say it:
I hate people!

ONE

THE TEN
LEAST WANTED

"Hell is — other people."

— Jean-Paul Sartre

We've been taught since we were kids that there are positive role models in our lives, and that by focusing on how they live their lives and what they teach us, we'll be better people.

But no one's really taught us what to do about the people who trip us up, siphon off our time, or send us off in the wrong direction. There's the guy assigned to your team who seems to know it all, but is actually a Know-It-None. There's Minute Man, who says he only needs a minute, then sucks up fifteen. And there's the coworker you're expecting to green-light your project who turns out to be a Stop Sign.

Welcome to the Ten Least Wanted, the main adversaries of the Soloist. Our better self. The person with the dual talent of working effectively with small groups as well as flying solo. Our goal is to show you the way to sharpen your skills as a People Hater. By doing so, you will become a better Soloist.

That's what it's all about. Productive hating.

The heart of our book is an exploration of the Soloist and the way he works best: Solocrafting. But before you can possibly hope to become a Soloist, first you have to face the reality of modern business. That's where the Ten Least Wanted comes in.

To succeed as a Soloist, you must first learn to vanquish your enemies.

> *It is said that if you know your enemies and know your-*
> *self, you will not be imperiled in a hundred battles.*
> — SUN TZU, *THE ART OF WAR*

People disappoint. Daily. Hourly. Why not wise up and get ready for it? The sooner you learn to stop getting sucker-punched and letting yourself get pissed off, the sooner you can get back to doing your own thing, your own way. So to help you identify these clowns and clods in the corporate sphere – and get on with your work – we've removed the guesswork. We've selected and analyzed the ten most troublesome people you'll encounter in the workplace.

The Ten Least Wanted are not created equal. Depending on your career and profession, some will be more endemic to your business. Every company is unique. As you meet the Ten Least Wanted on the following pages, you may find some personality types more familiar than others. One thing we can guarantee: virtually no company will ever be free of some of these people.

Some of these characters, in small doses and correctly aligned with your project goals, can aid instead of hold you back. The same guy who may one day hold up your budget – the Spreadsheet – may another day help you get the funding your project needs. The same loud, abrasive boss who regularly tests your resilience (a Bulldozer, perhaps) may also have the fortitude to keep your company sailing through hard times. And as perfect and smart as we all are, here's another truth we all know, whether we admit it publicly or not: even during your best week, you may find yourself playing a few of these Least Wanted roles yourself.

For the benefit of those who care about the inner workings of Stumbling Blocks and the rest of the Ten Least Wanted, we asked David Johnson, a British psychologist and the CEO of Venture to Think, to give us his "Psych Shot," a quick, one-line psychological profile. You'll find it right up top for each of our Ten Least Wanted.

Get to know these archetypes. Develop strategies to deflect and deal with them. You'll increase the time and space you need to Solocraft and become the Soloist of your dreams.

2. Stumbling Blocks

Meet the Stumbling Blocks, the men and women we call Stop Signs, Flimflams, and Bulldozers. This is the group that often wields the most power over your Solocrafting. They can tell you what to do, when to do it, and how to do it. They can be peers just as easily as bosses. They can be debilitating to new ventures and teams, and especially to your efforts to succeed as a Soloist. Stumbling Blocks can stop your project cold or send you spinning off on tasks that eat up weeks or months of your time.

1. Stop Sign

STEREOTYPE: Former Kodak executive: "Digital cameras will never catch on."

PSYCH SHOT: "Ridden by fear. Driven by detail. Behind fear lies his own uncertainty."

Stop Signs have cut short more careers and ruined more lives than probably any other downers in history.

Count on a Stop Sign to pour cold water on your every ambition.

Stop Signs can come from the top of your organization, like, say, the otherwise brilliant founder of Digital Equipment Corporation, Kenneth Olsen, who had the misfortune to announce in 1977 – just a year after the birth of Apple Computer – "There is no reason anyone would want a computer in their home." It was the beginning of the end for DEC, which missed out on the personal computer revolution – and sadly was later bought by Compaq, a PC maker.

Or they can be mentors like Fred Smith's Yale professor, who warned him that the premise of his paper on developing an overnight delivery company didn't seem feasible. Smith went on to found Federal Express. Then there are Stop Signing companies like Decca Records, which auditioned two bands on January 1, 1962. Decca gave the first the boot: "We don't like their sound, and guitar music is on the way out." Instead, Decca signed up the second band, reasoning that since the Tremeloes were local, the company would save considerable travel expenses.

That band Decca tried to stop cold? The Beatles.

"Any fool can criticize, condemn, and complain — and most fools do."

— BENJAMIN FRANKLIN

Historically, Stop Signs were responsible for such brilliant observations as "The world is flat" and "I think you've had enough fun" and "You'll put an eye out with that thing." Read biographies, and you'll find that at nearly every turn, great men and women faced Stop Signs who told them they wouldn't make it – as executives, actors, or even presidents (if only some had listened). Certain professionals specialize in Stop Sign thinking – lawyers and accounting firms, to name a couple. Stop Signs often masquerade as the wise and justify their negativity by the amount of time it saves them from thinking. A common example of corporate-wide Stop Signing over the past two decades has been company bans on Apple computers.

Stop Signs are often the most difficult nuts of the Ten Least Wanted to crack. Like a petulant two-year-old, their favorite response tends to be "No," leaving you with little in the way of a toehold to get any leverage to reason with them. One female executive despairs every time she has to deal with a chronic Stop Sign in her company: "He's the one who always says we can't do something." She's tried everything over the years, from the "attracting flies with honey" approach to doing a complete end around to disagreeing right to his face. Since *her* default personality is to be positive, energetic, and enthusiastic, she's never sure how to counter his attitude. Even when the Stop Sign purports to sign on to a project and his responsibilities are clear, he throws on the brakes unless commanded by a superior. The female executive's most successful tack: gaining the support of his boss – or his team – against his opposition.

But it can be a tough road, and she's learned the hard

way: if you don't run a stubborn Stop Sign early, he can derail your entire project.

Carl Haney, a Procter & Gamble man or, as we like to say, a VP in R&D at P&G, views Stop Signs as "exception hunters." "They'll point out the exceptions when I'm onto something good, saying, 'We tried it before, it didn't work.'"

Haney counters these Stop Signs by explaining that his idea has a good chance because it's facing "different circumstances and different competitors." Experienced innovators know that it takes years for genuinely new products to find markets. Stop Signs forget that what failed before might very well succeed now.

Stop Signs thrive in meetings. If you think of company meetings as a baseball game, holding up a Stop Sign is the easiest way to slap out a single. It takes far more creative firepower to offer a "build," to take a rough idea and suggest how you might cross it with something else or adapt it to make it work. But holding up that red sign does prove you aren't dead, and it's often wrapped in a protective tone: "Isn't that going to be expensive? . . . We haven't really sold products like that before. . . . How can we market that?"

One manager we spoke with said he's frequently faced with the standard Stop Signage: "Well, we could do it if we just had more time or resources." His technique is to listen carefully to his team's objections, and pick them apart one by one. If resources are the obstacle, he'll say, "Let's go to the program manager and see if we can get it." It's not that it can't be done, he says. "It's just that they're resistant to finding out how to do it."

Stop Signs are often managers or bosses, which is why the smartest companies in the world often bar them from early project meetings. Stop Signs, thinking they're adding to the creativity, strangle the wild ideas that frequently sprout from the free-form interchange in healthy brainstorms. What can you do? Deftly change the rules.

Pete Johnson, chief architect of Hewlett-Packard's website, HP.com, has many, many jobs that demand his attention, including the responsibility for developing the technology standards for all of the tech giant's websites. He says that when he's confronted with Stop Signs, he acknowledges the challenge – and takes it off the table: "Hey, I realized that's going to be a restriction. Let's be free of that for the morning." Repeat offenders are banned from meetings.

And if you can't keep the Stop Signs out, try holding up the verbal equivalent of a detour sign. When Bob says, "But we haven't the budget for that," respond with, "Let's pretend we've got the budget. Let's imagine that's not an obstacle."

Or co-opt Stop Sign's opposition: "Good point, Bob. How would you brainstorm three ways we could pay for the project?"

Haney of P&G often pushes in the opposite direction of the Stop Signs. Where they anticipate failure, he invites an exploration of a wild success. If a new product concept would need to earn a hundred million dollars in annual revenue to become a reality – a goal that now seems impossible – in a brainstorm he'll push the group to imagine a world far beyond that marker: "What would we have to do to make it a billion-dollar hit?"

Smart storytelling can help overcome Stop Signs. Think of your own parents, who, more likely than not, have begun to ossify into a couple of Stop Signs as they've gotten older. Bryan Mekechuk, an international management consultant, realized several years ago that every time he told his father he had a new idea, his dad would give him the Five Reasons It Will Fail. Mekechuk cleverly turned this into a story that almost anyone could understand. He flipped his father's negativity into an invitation for creativity: "Dad, tell me the ten things I have to do to make it work." Now when Mekechuk launches a new project, he works hard with the company to identify the potential human roadblocks. He tells the story about his dad, then says, "When we're dealing with this Stop Sign [at the company], we'll have to pry out the ten things we need to do to go forward."

Mekechuk says that the simple technique works. It's a way of acknowledging that Stop Signs are everywhere.

We believe in the adage "A strong defense is a good offense." Preemptive strikes work wonders. A product marketing vice president suggests loading your shotgun before the showdown. "Build consensus prior to a decision meeting, where you've got everyone saying yes and you know this person's going to say no." Once the big meeting hits, "you've already presold everyone. You've got nine out of ten people nodding their heads." Unless the Stop Sign has an incredibly compelling argument or veto power, the idea will usually survive.

That said, there are times when tougher measures may be required. When the nastiest of Stop Signs craps all over your latest brainchild, don't take it personally. Try calmly replying, "What's *your* new idea?"

2. Flimflam

STEREOTYPES: On a good day, Danny Ocean (George Clooney, *Ocean's Eleven*); on a bad day, Lester "Worm" Murphy (Edward Norton, *Rounders*).

PSYCH SHOT: "Manipulative. Often Machiavellian. Gets others to feather his nest. Likes to be liked. Expert at identifying people to do his bidding."

Sharp but somewhat casual dresser. Keeps spotty office hours, justifying his absence with vague claims of client trips, trade shows, and off-sites.

Flimflam is smooth at feeding you a story and getting you to sign off on it. He has a project he needs you to do. It's easy, he says. All you need to do is go to a few client meetings. How do you know you're dealing with a Flimflam? He wants you to make a commitment. Speed up delivery dates. Double the feature set. Expand the services. He's short on details. Why? Because he's really got a lot in common with his criminal cousin the con man – only his currency is your time and productivity.

The forgiving sort never expect larceny in Flimflam's soul. But honestly, the difference is just one of degree. Like the criminal version, Flimflam takes. Only here it's more than money. Flimflam can sometimes take all of your time, saddling you with a horrific project for weeks or months.

Just as a con man rarely leaves his card, Flimflam eschews details. The project is such a sure thing that he either wants to tell you about it in person or shoot you a quick e-mail. A master of peer pressure, Flimflam will talk about doing things for the team or the company. He'll often rope one of his disciples into playing the witness, being in the room to hear you say yes to this nightmare. Because really, he's trying to sell you a shiny car that you'll soon learn had a bad valve job and its odometer dialed back.

Some companies have a management style that encourages Flimflammery. As one former suffering employee anonymously posted at Yahoo/Finance, "I spent many years at Microsoft. There, managers deliberately overloaded workers with tasks because the logic was that the most important tasks would automatically rise to the top, and the ones that you never got to, well, those were clearly not that important, and eventually whoever requested the task would either change it, revise it, or forget about it."

There's a problem with this institutional shell game. It's all passive, increasing the odds that there will be lots of nasty misunderstandings and mistakes about just what is or isn't important.

The Flimflam tries to take advantage of your ability. "A lot of times, these people are always depending on me for their deliverables," says Vernon Hurd, a systems analyst for DG FastChannel, an advertising distribution firm. "They want me to help them do *their* work." He throws the requests back on the Flimflams, offering to help them out just so long as they realize the consequences. If he helps them do the work they should have done in the first place, it's going to take extra time – a delay that has to be accounted for. Hurd makes clear that higher-ups will know he's covering for them. "That's when they realize they have to do the work themselves."

Shelly, a project manager for a medium-size firm, said her office Flimflam excels at taking his victims by surprise. "He'll always try to talk to me in passing. As if it wasn't even worth having a real meeting over. He's just gotten off the phone with the client or had an in-house meeting." His classic pitch was the age-old line of the Flimflam: "Could you work on this project? It's a really small, quick thing. No big deal."

After repeatedly being burned with his disastrous, lengthy Flimflam projects, Shelly learned not to sign on right away. She began to ask detailed questions. The Flimflam would feign ignorance and try to minimize things. But putting him off worked wonders. He's left her alone for a really long time. She laughs: "He had to get somebody else to do his work."

One high-tech executive we spoke to has found that one of the latest Flimflam tricks is to IM people to do his dirty work during a meeting. "I work with this woman. We'll be on a phone meeting, and instead of raising the controversial point herself, she'll IM everybody else to try to get them to do it." He's dubbed her the Ventriloquist, and says she fooled him twice. He put an end to it when he realized she never climbed out on the limb herself. What does he do now? He IMs the Flimflam right back: "You really should do that."

Your best defense against a Flimflam's demand that you hop to some task: sleep on it, and then counter the Flimflam with clarity. Flimflams want to keep things as hazy as a summer afternoon.

Ask for a page detailing the project, an estimate of the tasks, and the time required. The best Flimflams try to talk it up on the phone or in person. Push back. You need to see it in writing. That's when they'll probably slide their thin con job down the hallway for a more naive victim. If they do respond in writing, push back, if for no other reason than that once Flimflams make you for a mark, you can guarantee they'll be back with more hellish projects.

3. Bulldozer

Stereotype: Tony Soprano (James Gandolfini, *The Sopranos*): "A wrong decision is better than indecision."

PSYCH SHOT: "Defense mechanism. He, too, has been bulldozed. Dominating. Prone to bashing the table. Creates a resentful dependency."

Why do so many companies have successful, entrenched Bulldozers? Because most people aren't willing to stand up to these clods. It's hard. It can be painful and downright dangerous. We all remember playground bullies. When these people graduate to the office environment, they find even more people to stomp on. Where once they could dominate a handful of people, now they may smack around dozens or hundreds.

Many Bulldozers fall into the class of what's now considered workplace bullies, who appear to be thriving on both sides of the Atlantic. A recent Columbia University study revealed that nine out of ten workers are roughed up by bosses sooner or later, while a British study chalked up eighteen million lost work days a year to bullies (victims miss an extra week of work per year, on average). The Brits, who take office misbehaving seriously, say the worst abuse resembles post-traumatic stress disorder. Even here in the bully-friendly U.S., Bullybusters.org claims that more than a third of victims of company bullies end up clinically depressed.

But since Bulldozers are not always bullies or outright jerks – and are often less outrageously offensive – expect little or no help from human resources or management. Official action frequently comes only after years of damage. Consider the Nebraska firm where a manager regularly got plastered at lunch and then verbally abused his staff. After HR and senior management did nothing for a year, the offender swore repeatedly in front of ten staffers. Only when the ten victims of the abuse filed written statements, documenting the abuse, did the company bother to take action.

While some experts recommend pressing the "ignore" button, that only works if the Bulldozer isn't your boss or your interactions are minimal.

If you start to feel as though you're getting plowed under, consider the course advocated by a North Carolina network administrator who learned from his air force lieutenant colonel dad, "You should keep a record, in writing, of everything." He kept a phone log and found it provided a backup, ultimately protecting him from a boss who believed that all directions should be "short and dirty." He kept his "dignity and self-respect intact," while the boss got the reprimand he deserved.

Bulldozers foolish enough to shove you around in e-mails leave their own self-incriminating paper trail. The key is to stand up with tough but not incendiary responses. "Unreasonable" is a good word, as is the phrase "I won't be pushed around." If you have allies within the company, blind carbon-copy (BCC) the chain of correspondence to your manager or coworkers.

But most Bulldozers aren't backed off by a few e-mails. If he keeps running over you in person, sometimes you've got to put a stop to it. Pick your time and place and consider playing the "Team" card. An IT professional says that when the Bulldozer aggressively trashes your presentation in a meeting, stop cold in your tracks, pause, and, in a calm voice, say, "Since you don't want to be a team player, and you aren't providing any solutions, I'd prefer it if you would step out until I finish my presentation."

The IT man says it works every time.

There are also thousands of Bulldozers who pose a more

subtle challenge. They're men and women with what Carl Haney of P&G calls "a high share of voice in a meeting." They may not be bullies, but all the same, these bigmouthed Bulldozers may dominate the discussion and divert your agenda. And often they're so enamored of the sound of their own bullhorn that they can't articulate a specific point of view.

Pin the Bulldozer down, says Haney, with a very direct question: "Do you have a recommendation?"

Sadly, Bulldozers are not only fellow workers and bosses. They may also be customers or clients. Consider Marc van Gerven, an executive in the solar-power industry, who, when getting his start as a manager at General Electric, discovered that a lot of its high-tech drilling-equipment customers were disgruntled. The situation had deteriorated to the point that many GE people didn't even want to face the customers. Van Gerven took a different tack. He hired a salesman to meet with the clients in Houston and Calgary. He acknowledged the problems and let his clients know that the company was starting the hard work to fix them. That's when he really found himself nearly plowed under.

"Some customers were Bulldozers," he says. "They realized the louder they screamed, the faster they'd get a part. Then they'd brag to their competitors: 'Hey, I just got one!'" And not just that. "Some Bulldozers were getting steep discounts and boasting about that too."

Van Gerven decided, *No more.* He told every client – including the Bulldozers – his or her place on the product delivery list. There would be no more favoritism. He had to stick up for his "No Bulldozers" rule. It got worse before it got better. "Once we stopped reacting to the screaming," van Gerven says, "they screamed louder and louder." After several months, there were signs of improvement. By then, GE had introduced a more realistic, transparent delivery system. The Bulldozers told van Gerven that GE would fail. The screaming gradually subsided. After a year, the Bulldozers had been stopped in their tracks.

As we've seen, it requires courage to take a stand. Few coworkers will join hands with you against a raging Bulldozer. Sure, they'll complain about the Bulldozer behind his back and gossip about his latest tirade: "Can you believe he screamed in the hallway?" What's missing in these stories? No one ever calls Bulldozer on his crap. These same coworkers also often talk about how the Bulldozer had a bad week or rough day. They're Bulldozer enablers.

What they fail to see is that Bulldozers aren't as intimidating as they seem. To begin with, they're only effective when they're on solid ground. Ground that you can take away.

Make Bulldozer spin his big fat treads in the sand. Next time he swears or heaves a phone book, call it out. Point out that he's swearing or yelling, and leave the room. Or end the call.

Remember: You're the adult dealing with a tantrum. No wise parent gives in to a child's fit because it just leads to more fits.

You're wrapping Bulldozer's fury with tough love. By making statements about his conduct, you're putting him on notice. Keep up your game, and by the second or third attempt, Bulldozer will tire of spinning his treads in the sand. His inner bully will tell him that you are winning these verbal wrestling matches. He's getting the message. Time to move on to more scrawny victims.

That's the funny thing about Bulldozers. Take away the dirt, and they can't really plow you under.

3. Wrong Turns

Of all the characters likely to bruise you in a company, none may be more dangerous than Wrong Turns. Entire books have been written on one flavor of Stumbling Blocks: Bullies and Bulldozers. Here we're talking about something far more subtle.

While it's easy to spot a Bulldozer or an asshole, Wrong Turns excel at corporate deception, a far more pervasive and troubling problem in many organizations. Worst of all, these very same people may be praised for their skills in manipulating the many human cogs that clog most enterprises. Far from viewing them as bullies or jerks, the boss may view them as corporate jewels. They are likely to be peers with the power to mess with your career on a daily basis.

Wrong Turns can send you sliding into the ditch. Skidding off the cliff. Push you off on tangents that sabotage key projects and assignments. They are the Smiley Face,

Liar Liar, and Switchblade. Forget the nice-guy, psycho-babble nonsense of trying to understand their pain. You have a job to do. Learn to see them coming, or you'll spend so much time watching your back that you'll find it all but impossible to keep things moving forward.

4. Smiley Face

STEREOTYPES: The Joker (*Batman*); politicians, office managers, bank clerks, and human skulls.

PSYCH SHOT: "Behavior designed to avoid pain, sadness, and distress."

Today, a smile is hardly a guarantee of happiness. When you see that guy at work, grinning like a jack-o'-lantern and heading your way, there's a good chance he's got something nasty up his sleeve. Problem is, Smiley Face smiles pretty much all the time. You've got no clue what he's thinking.

Back in caveman days, a smile was a challenge. Teeth bared in raw, savage, animalistic imitation of much larger and more dangerous predators. Keep that in mind the next time that crescent of teeth comes at you. It will make it much easier to recall that the brain behind the molars is likely up to no good.

Come to think of it, looking at photographs dating back just fifty years ago, smiling wasn't very in vogue. Lots of stern faces, from photos of industry titans and world leaders to family portraits. If you were happy, you damn well kept it to yourself.

So how can you tell if that friendly office grin is real?

Dr. Paul Ekman, the University of California, San Francisco, professor of psychology who has assisted the CIA and FBI in reading the facial cues of criminals and terrorists, says that when it's a fake, the only thing that moves is the zygomatic major muscle – the muscle that runs from the cheekbone to the corner of the lips. As Ekman told the *New York Times,* "In a real smile, the eyebrows and the skin between the upper eyelid and the eyebrow come down very slightly. The muscle involved is the orbicularis oculi, pars lateralis."

Translation: If the eyebrows and eyelids don't move, watch out: it's a phony smile!

There's definitely something creepy about people who can't stop smiling. One executive describes Smiley Faces as "the super-happy people that kind of freak you out. You're skeptical about their motives and you're waiting for the other shoe to drop. I don't have time for people who are fake. Trying to get something out of you. The ones that put on a mask."

The trick is finding out if that smile is to be trusted. "My hackles go up," a director of marketing tells us about her company's human resources director. "I deal with her. But she makes me uncomfortable, and I can't figure out what she wants." Research has shown there are three basic smiles: genuine, false, and disdainful. In today's corporate world, plastic smiles abound. One is the thin veneer stretched tight over the face of a desperate man. Someone who wants – no, needs – your help to get out of some kind of jam. Avoid at all costs. This smile is like the arms of a drowning man, and may only pull you under.

Then there's the smile of disdain or contempt. The grin you'll frequently get in response to a question. Sneery, with a hint of superiority. When you're looking for honest feedback, the last thing you need is Smiley Face giving you a blank and vacuous gaze. That is when that smirk isn't leering or downright feral – gleeful at seeing you in a fresh predicament.

The perpetual happy face can't disguise underhanded behavior for long. "I had to deal with one of these clowns," one corporate cube dweller told us. "It wasn't just the smiling that drove everyone crazy; it was his habit of smiling while twisting the knife to get people fighting one another. He had a special ability to invent tensions between coworkers, a greasy smile that looked like it belonged on a used-car salesman." Coupled with an ingratiating tone of voice, "that ass-kissing smile seemed custom-designed to make normal folks want to butcher him."

Smiley Faces are often bad news. For instance, your boss may be a Smiley Face as he tells you to undertake some huge project – or hands you your pink slip. Smiley Face can also be a cube neighbor who seems to be a happy-go-lucky guy . . . till the day that sunny smile informs you that he's moving to a private office because he got that promotion you were counting on.

Unlike the other Ten Least Wanted, there is no proven strategy to combat Smiley Face, except perhaps calling him on it. Especially when things are rough: the team just missed its deadline, or your budget was cut. Try calmly saying, "What are you smiling about?"

There's no guarantee you'll get an answer, but at least you've begun the process of cracking that veneer.

Whatever you do, make sure you don't attempt to outsmile

Smiley Face. It's a trap. Not only will it prove impossible, but you may seriously injure muscles in your face and neck.

5. Liar Liar

STEREOTYPE: Tommy Flanagan, Jon Lovitz's pathological-liar character from *Saturday Night Live:* "Yeah, that's the ticket!"

PSYCH SHOT: "Insecure and uncertain. Not able to be honest because of a lack of confidence. Wants to be liked. Hides behind lies to make himself feel okay."

Lying is endemic in corporate America. Research by the psychologist Gerald Jellison suggests that we may encounter up to as many as two hundred lies a day. While we may think that extreme figure is limited to the government, one in five workers freely admits to lying at least once a week. More than 95 percent of college students are willing to lie to get a job. Studies are showing that lies and deceptions have been on the uptick. People lie at work about results, performance, accomplishments, values, and motives.

In a large corporation, it can be tricky to catch Liar Liar at his game. Artfully crafted fibs, stories, and half-truths make for a wily character. Adept at squirming out of commitments, deadlines, and performance reviews, Liar Liar justifies his lies by the lies others tell in his business or other industries. When he finally gets cornered, Liar Liar will often skillfully blame someone else.

The most common fakeout may be the one used to get

out of the undesirable business trip. "This is where the salesman has been ordered to go to Kansas for a dreadful sales meeting," says Art Bell, executive director for MBA programs at the University of San Francisco and coauthor of *Winning with Trust in Business*. "The salesman will tell his boss his kid has a serious medical condition, and he has to take him to a specialist." Bell notes that along with being a bald-faced lie, this sort of lie spawns more lies, such as when the boss asks how the son is doing. It can also get the salesman fired when the boss asks the wife at the company party about her ailing son, and she brags about him having made the Junior Olympic fencing team.

> "Everybody lies — every day; every hour; awake; asleep; in his dreams; in his joy; in his mourning; if he keeps his tongue still, his hands, his feet, his eyes, his attitude, will convey deception."
>
> — MARK TWAIN

One of the reasons the workplace breeds Liar Liars is that it's so easy to spin the little lies. The inconsistencies of technology aid and abet the Liar Liar: "I never got that e-mail" or "You didn't get any of my voice mails?" or "My hard drive crashed." Thanks to our modern conveniences, this BS has never been so easy. There are endless ways to cook up a good, believable "The dog ate my homework" scenario. And many figure that the ends justify the means. By offering a phony reason why they didn't do something, they look at it as one less thing to worry about.

If you're not mindful of Liar Liar, he may keep his tap-dancing double-talk going right up until the point when he's out the door and gone, never having been held accountable. "We had an accounts-payable guy like that," says Jennifer Cooke, a West Coast marketing executive. "Our regular person was out on medical leave, and this guy was a temp we'd hired in the interim." Complaints about missing invoices, checks, and receipts fell on deaf ears until, eventually, the Liar Liar left and the regular accountant returned – and the money was gone. "It was only then we realized how much the wool had been pulled over our eyes."

> Twenty to thirty percent of middle managers have written fraudulent internal reports.
>
> — *Fortune*

If you think you've got a good BS detector, think again: research has shown that for most of us, the odds of ferreting out a lie are no better than guessing the result of a coin toss. If you've got the budget, consider hiring a former Secret Service agent for the tough cases: they nail the liar four out of five times.

Fortunately, training may improve your office detection skills. Like the poker player who always bluffs, Liar Liar has his "tells" that reveal he's spinning a whopper. A lot of research has been done on the subject of Liar Liar's giveaways by folks like Allan and Barbara Pease, authors of *The Definitive Book of Body Language.* We discovered that there are more signs that a lie is being perpetrated than baseball coaches have signals. Here's a brief sample from the Peases' book.

Liar Liar "Tells"

Touching the nose
Rubbing the eyes
Scratching the neck
Excessive sweating
Pupils dilating
Sideways glance
Playing with hair
Excessive blinking
Tugging the earlobe
Pulling the collar

Research has also shown that squirrelly tactics – delays in answering a question, withholding information, ambivalence, repetition, and not taking responsibility – are signs of deceit. Liars tend to repeat subtle details of their lie, says Martha Davis, PhD, who has worked with homicide detectives – pros at rooting out falsehoods – for more than a decade.

As you can see by these evasive behaviors and list of tells, almost all of us are Liar Liars once in a while. But what you need to look for are the people who are habitual, chronic, or terminal in their twitches. Keep watching for these and the other telltale tells, and with a little analysis, you will learn to spot these and many other clues revealing Liar Liars.

Of course, if all else fails, try the squeak test. Ray Hyman, a professor of psychology at the University of Oregon and a renowned critic of crackpot ideas – namely, parapsychology – says that mind readers can put their subject in a squeaky chair. "The person may not be saying anything, but the squeaks tell you when you're hitting a nerve," says

The Most Common Office Lies

· ·

▷ I don't know how that happened.

▷ I have another call to take.

▷ I've been out of town or out sick.

▷ I like your outfit, or you look great.

— CareerBuilder.com

Hyman. It follows that you can grill your suspected Liar Liar in a rusty desk chair and see if you can get the chair to squeal. Chances are, the louder it squeaks, the more likely he's lying.

The more realistic approach is to plan on workplace lies, and simply start building a paper or e-mail trail to protect yourself from suspected Liar Liars. The more bits and pieces of correspondence you have that help prove the truth behind an incident, the more ammo you have when it comes time for a showdown.

A less confrontational method is to drop a hint, a casual aside in conversation. Experts love the euphemistic phrase *"truth encouragement"* (aka "Stop lying!"). This gives people a second chance: "Bob, help me understand these numbers . . ." or "Is there another way we might look at this?"

Sometimes, when they know they're busted, Liar Liars will make a clean breast of things if it gets them off the hook. When it's your word against his, Liar Liar may not wilt so easily, which means you'll have to dig in your heels and prepare for a grudge match.

When disarming a Liar Liar, we suggest bringing along a second – an ally to serve as witness and backup if the fibber goes ballistic. State your case. Lay out your evidence. Give him a chance to defend his actions. You're not looking for an enemy – or turning a Liar Liar into a Switchblade (see below). But you're making it clear that you see his lies coming a mile away. He's unlikely to turn over a new leaf, but he knows the price has gone up for trying to put one over on you.

6. Switchblade

STEREOTYPE: JUDAS.

PSYCH SHOT: "Resentful. Vindictive. Childish. Under stress, switches from rescuer to persecutor."

Difficult to see coming, Switchblades are tricky. You might think of them as friends, only to find out something has turned them against you. And not just in a way that makes them hate you, but to the extent that they mean to do you harm.

The Switchblade can damage your image, reputation, or ego. The knife might be slipped in subtly, over weeks or months, or slammed in abruptly, fueled by a sudden rage in response to some perceived slight. The only thing you can be sure of is that you'll rarely see it coming. You've got to figure out who the Switchblade is and what to do about him before he strikes.

Ever been hanging out with someone from the office, maybe knocking back a couple of beers, and he starts trashing people from work? Heck, maybe you're both doing it – it *is* a time-honored pastime. Except you notice that not only are *his* remarks pointed and barbed, but he seems to have a bad word for everyone. Except you. His buddy. His drinking pal. How did you escape this hornet's sting? Easy: you didn't.

He's a Switchblade! And next week, when it's someone else he's having beers with, you can bet your head will be on the chopping block along with everyone else's.

Shrug it off? Possibly. But what if next week's confidant happens to be the boss? Who, informally of course, would love the Switchblade to give his impression of his staff.

Some of us are lucky to have a boss parry the thrust of a Switchblade. One technique is to snap the blade with a reply-all e-mail blast. "I had a woman who tried to throw me under the bus when I was on vacation," says Tania, an advertising executive for a major firm. "My boss – who's a straight shooter – forwarded me the e-mail where this woman literally was saying I wasn't doing my job. My boss knew something was fishy, so she copied everybody with her reply – including me – asking if anyone else wanted to speak up about my work performance." Her rival's plan backfired and, needless to say, Tania won.

Several executives we talked to said the toughest personal obstacle can be the manager or executive who is smiling and nodding her head, and seems to be saying "Yes, yes, yes" while actually thinking "No, no, no." As one industry leader put it, "The Switchblade can sucker you in and end up screwing you big time. You really have to make sure you understand their real position. You've got to probe and talk to them. You've got to get them to say no when they've been saying yes."

The Soloist is a realist. Some companies are rife with

Switchblades. If that's the lay of this land, make a choice. Does the career opportunity outweigh the political infighting? If not, consider walking away – and starting something new. You may be surprised at how many people join you.

Consider the challenge Dorian Banks faced when he was hired by Voith, a large private German company, to help launch a series of major technical innovations across the wide-flung enterprise. A Canadian, Banks was used to the standard corporate process: major meetings, making a decision, then moving forward with the implementation. That didn't happen in Germany. "There'd be these big time lags: a one-week project would turn into six weeks. It was dumbfounding. I didn't believe it was happening." Banks had to make repeated lengthy phone calls or return to the various offices, saying, "Did you understand what we'd decided to do?" E-mail was worthless: "Response to e-mail in countries like Germany is, like, a week. It's just another note that's deletable."

Six months into this tortuous project, Banks finally realized that he wasn't just being thwarted by Stop Signs. He was being knifed by a Switchblade.

Banks happened to overhear one of his program decisions being talked about: "He's not going to do that..." Banks was incredulous. He had thought the man in question, friendly and agreeable in meetings, was completely onboard. The last person he would have suspected was sabotaging his efforts.

Banks confronted the Switchblade in person. "Oh, no, I wouldn't do that," said the blade right to his face, smiling.

In a perfect world, Banks might have tried to transform the Switchblade. But the deadline was too tight. He had to formally exclude the man from the project. Then: an attack by another Switchblade. The head of an entire division openly refused to adopt the new changes. This was open rebellion. Banks had to call in a higher-level executive and play hardball. "I had to have a letter sent to the head of the division [saying] that he'd lose his job if he didn't enforce my programs," Banks says. "It wasn't easy."

Switchblades catch you by surprise. Recognize that they exist – and start coming up with a plan to take away their edge.

Sometimes you can switch a Switchblade. A few years ago, Amabel Garcia, a learning solutions specialist for AAA, found one of her team members twisting the knife. The Switchblade started dissing her writing abilities to other team members. Even more challenging, Garcia had to supervise the San Francisco team remotely, from Las Vegas.

It's not always easy to keep tabs on your crew when they're five hundred miles away, but someone else on the team had Garcia's back and let her know what was going on. On her next visit, she confronted the Switchblade directly, which shocked him. Explaining that her organizational and leadership skills – and not her writing ability – were the key to her job, Garcia handily recruited the Switchblade to take on the team's writing responsibilities. Now she's got an ally instead of an enemy. Instead of grumbling, the former Switchblade is able to shine.

4. Time Wasters

We've all been sold the con that instant messaging, e-mail, and texting are going to save time and make us more productive. Well, it hasn't happened yet, so let's consider a new path: dealing with the human element slowing us down at every turn. The Time Wasters.

At first glance, they don't pose the same threat as Wrong Turns or Stumbling Blocks. Time Wasters won't betray you like a Switchblade or crush you like a Bulldozer. They don't want your job. They generally aren't nasty. They may even believe they have your best interests at heart. But trust us: they're on Satan's road crew, as in "The road to hell is paved with good intentions."

Time Wasters steal your most valuable possession bit by bit. Grabbing seconds that add up to hours and weeks and, over a lifetime, years. Minute Man, Know-It-None, and Spreadsheet just want to tell you a story, or get your input, or make you jump through senseless hoops. They can't help themselves. And if you don't help yourself, you'll be losing chunks of time better spent Solocrafting.

7. Minute Man

STEREOTYPE: Lieutenant Columbo (Peter Falk, *Columbo*): "I don't mean to bother you, but I just have one more question . . ."

PSYCH SHOT: "Control freak. Issues with trust. Never delegates."

Never underestimate the Minute Man. Highly dangerous because he's got you before you realize you've been had. Expert at slicing off increasingly larger hunks of your time. What's worse is that these people run the gamut from coworkers and customers to complete strangers. All they want is a minute of your time. And another minute . . . And then just one more minute . . . If you're not careful, you'll end up without a second left to yourself.

Minute Men can be the most unlikely suspects, the people you thought were going to save you time – folks like your admin or secretary. Newbies often seem to need a minute every other minute, as they try to figure out how the copy machine works, how to reserve the conference room, and why that perfectly good password they had at their previous job won't get them on the network.

One executive we spoke to has seen his share of Minute Men, the employees who burn time and constantly require reassurance. He's developed two different strategies. He isolates Minute Men so they're less of a drain on the company. Or he repositions the person: in one case, he was able to flip a Minute Woman who was driving him nuts. "She'd check in on everything. Over and over again. I decided to give her the new job of calling on customers. Helping with our collections. Signing up customers for classes."

This is the best possible outcome: converting an irritant into an asset.

On the other hand, if you're too forgiving, you might fall into the trap of letting Minute Man steal away your precious minutes, say, by having you show him how to do things. Next thing you know, your status is draining away as fast as your time. *Why is he putting toner in the copier? Isn't that the intern's job?*

Here are a couple of tricks to reclaim your minutes. An oldie but goodie: make a show of checking your cell phone or watch. The pressing engagement works equally well. "I've been guilty of making up things that I have to go do," a product-development executive told us. He and others confess to the standard ploy of saying they have to cut one meeting short because of another. But tread lightly. If you're not careful, you just may find yourself resembling one of the worst of the Ten Least Wanted: Liar Liar.

Instead, try one of the last things that comes to mind: generosity. Tell Minute Man that you've got a full two minutes, but then you've got to run. You'll burn less time and make fewer enemies.

Skilled executives have long been masters of the "hard stop." This is the preemptive strike, invented by an executive (name withheld) who didn't want to attend a meeting: "We have a hard stop at three p.m." Why limit this technique to meetings? Use the same language with Minute Man. Since you know damn well he's going to take more than a minute, be magnanimous. "We've got five minutes, Bob. That's the best I can do. I've got a hard stop at three thirty!"

The challenge is getting Minute Man to break his non-stop interruptions. AAA's Tasha Gibert prefers a straight approach. "I get them to give me all of the information up front, so they don't keep coming back," she says. "They're generally pretty responsive. I try to watch my tone. Because of my directness, I sometimes come across as being mean."

No reason to fear ruffling feathers. There's no such thing as being too direct with a Minute Man. This front-loading technique has been further refined by a public relations director for a premier resort chain. She tells her staff to start an e-mail in the morning and gradually put all their questions into it throughout the day. The catch: she instructs them not to send the e-mail until the end of the day, saving her a lot of time. "I look at it in the morning, put together the info they need, and take care of it all at once."

And sometimes you can nip the Minute Man in the earbud: at home, a dog may be man's best friend, but in the office, your best friend is a good set of headphones. While some companies still frown on their use, our research tells us that this, too, shall pass. (Consider how quickly headphones have become de rigueur for gym rats, joggers, and hikers.) "I always have headphones wherever I work. Even if I have an office," a startup executive told us, echoing a number of our interviews.

Dealing with a Minute Man is a work in progress. Don't worry about being abrupt or gruff: Minute Men are bulletproof. The one thing you can be certain about Minute Man is that he'll be back for more.

8. Know-It-None

STEREOTYPE: Cliff Clavin (John Ratzenberger, *Cheers*). Blaring voice. Can't tell the difference between fact and bullshit.

PSYCH SHOT: "Compulsion for friendships and relationships. Conflicts with people who want to work."

Everybody hates a know-it-all, but what's even worse is a Know-It-None. Those insufferable boobs with the booming voice and peanut-size brain. They are a wealth of facts, figures, and arcane knowledge, most of which is completely wrong.

Know-It-Nones infest the workplace, but there is no limitation on where these blowhards can ruin your day. When you're on a plane, they don't even have to be seated next to you to drive you nuts. They can be three rows back, spouting on and on, maddeningly ignorant regardless of the topic. Know-It-Nones love trivial positions of authority, and if they can't worm themselves into one at your company, you're sure to encounter them fronting some community group, or maybe your kid's sports team. Remarkably, otherwise intelligent people often take these bozos at face value without questioning their authority or knowledge.

The plague of Know-It-Nones has spread exponentially with the rise of the Internet. Wikipedia, Google, and millions of random blogs have become the arsenal of the misinformed, stuffing their heads with random nonsense that might be partly right but usually tends to be skewed, misinterpreted, or just dead wrong ("Is Google Making Us

Stupid?" was the title of a 2008 *Atlantic Monthly* article). These people have become trivia experts of the worst stripe, the most heinous of them addicts, regularly tapping out their inane Google queries and crowing out cockeyed answers to questions no one asked.

What if you are the unlucky cubemate of a Know-It-None? That was the bum card dealt a Wall Street trader we talked to. The Know-It-None told rambling, painfully long-drawn-out disaster stories from his days as a fireman. To make things worse, he made a point of delaying the punch line as long as possible. "The first three weeks, he drove me up the wall. A booming voice, unpolished. I'd let myself get suckered in to one anecdote or story after another." By the third week, "I'd just put my head down. Interrupt him midsentence: 'Look, I'm busy.'" The trader began to gradually add other outs – "I have to call somebody back . . . I need to get this done." Ultimately, the key turned out to be the first one out. "If you could break out early, it was easier."

Know-It-None presents an even larger danger in meetings by distorting situations and diverting focus. Deflate him by quickly asking, "What's your source on that? Did you get that from the Internet?" When Know-It-None fesses up that his source is garbage, issue a broad smile to undercut his nonsense. If he continues his bluster, suggest that it might be helpful to get some verifiable facts.

Make certain to cut short Know-It-None's incessant intrusions at your office or cube, so they don't become a habit. Showing him the back of your head can be surprisingly effective. If you're feeling talkative, try the long version – a one-word, noncommittal exclamation: "Interesting."

Then get back to work.

9. Spreadsheet

STEREOTYPE: Dr. Niles Crane (David Hyde Pierce, *Frasier*): "I'll have a double cappuccino, half-caf, nonfat milk, with enough foam to be aesthetically pleasing but not to leave me with a moustache."

PYSCH SHOT: "Obsessive. Terrified of losing control. Learned that if he steps out, he gets slapped. May have floundered when he didn't have control. Parents may have abandoned him."

Anal retentive. Favors muted tones in new clothes that always seem out of style.

Is there anyone who hasn't been Spreadsheeted? Spreadsheet is our designation for those by-the-book fanatics. They corrupt everyone with an overwrought sense of "The Rules," while simultaneously sucking all the fun and energy out of any endeavor. As one programmer put it, "They're the ones who'll micromanage you to death."

On the plus side, they're drawn toward positions that often shield the wily Soloist from excessive exposure. Number-loving Spreadsheets range from accountants to chief financial officers, while ironically, those with a "passion for people" become efficiency experts or excel at human resources, the professional People Haters. Come on: how could human resources folks *not* hate people? Their job requires them not only to put up with the Ten Least Wanted, but even to defend their behavior. And worst of all, they can't exhibit any of the natural responses the rest of us take for granted, such as "Stop whining!"

Don't breathe too easily. These narrow-visioneers occasionally burrow in with the rest of us. They believe they're bringing order and certainty. They can drain the life force out of projects and people.

Consider the case of a marketing director charged with maintaining the information on her company's website. Yet whenever she asked for something, the IT guy's standard reply was, "Sorry, no." The website contained the schedules and press information for three professional sports teams, major rock bands, and children's ice shows. "He blocked everyone from MySpace or online radio stations," she says, and when she told him she needed access, he said he *"couldn't"* do it. She complained to her boss. But even with him giving her backup, the IT continued to Spreadsheet her, saying, "It's too hard to reconfigure your computer." Accountants can be bad, but techies may be the worst. In the end, of course, with the marketing director's persistence, granting access proved doable.

The most common sign of an obsessive-compulsive Spreadsheet may be the irritatingly pristine desk and office. Beware of the Spreadsheet who volunteers to make your desk or all-important project space clean enough to eat off. Soloists need serendipity and chaos for ideas and thoughts to cascade into something new. Many of the best minds in business have some of the manic energy and output of a good comic. Spreadsheets freak out at the explosion of wild ideas and try to put a straitjacket on them.

Nothing wrong with an occasionally tidy workplace. But let that pressure infect your daily or hourly focus, and a subtle internal shift takes place. That Spreadsheet in a brainstorm who insists on writing down all the ideas spreads his malignancy. Your crack team becomes better at tracking ideas than at coming up with them.

What can a good Soloist do?

Strike a compromise. Make the kindergarten argument. During playtime (the workday), the toys come out, and yes, things will be gleefully disordered. As Bob the Spreadsheet gets ruffled, calmly explain, "That's the creative process, Bob. Studies at 3M showed that employees with a messy desk were three times more likely to invent new products. Don't you know this is how Thomas Edison did it?"

You promise to put most of the toys away at the end of the day. Not all, because you're not going to become a Spreadsheet, but enough so people can find the fire escape.

Vernon Hurd, the systems analyst who knew how to handle a Flimflam, has come up with the simple method of transference. He employs what he says one of his old fraternity brothers called the Jedi Mind Trick, a reference to the mystical powers of persuasion used by the Jedi Knights of *Star Wars*. "I make them think that my idea was their idea," he says.

Hurd says corporate IT people and their egos tend to get hung up on interface design – and go immediately on the defensive if changes are suggested. Recently, Hurd was trying to convince the IT department that it should implement live-chat support on the site: "The development manager was dead set against it. He thought it was too much work and couldn't see how people would benefit from chatting with someone through the site."

The Spreadsheet then told Hurd, "They'll just call like they do today."

Hurd let things lie for a few weeks, and sure enough, an opportunity came along in which he could apply the Jedi Mind Trick. The development manager was struggling to upload one of his presentations. For help, he turned to Hurd, who, using his Jedi powers, directed him to the "live chat" icon on-screen. The development manager clicked the button, and tech support joined in less than a minute and walked him through loading his presentation. The formerly skeptical manager was instantly transformed from Spreadsheet to evangelist. The next day, he was pitching live-chat support "as if it were a new idea based on his experience with the conferencing support," recalls Hurd. "His big selling point was that our support staff would be able to walk customers through their problems on-screen."

Hurd didn't care about who would receive the credit for the more advanced support system. He got what he wanted: "We started implementation the next week."

Master the Jedi Mind Trick, and you're ready to start saving the galaxy from Spreadsheets everywhere.

10. Sheeple

STEREOTYPE: Zombies (*Night of the Living Dead*).
Love meetings.

PSYCH SHOT: "Domineering parents. Learned to follow, not to ask questions. Avoids making decisions."

Welcome to the Vast Majority. Sheeple can be the most maddening, contentious, and difficult to outmaneuver. Why? Because these are the folks with advanced degrees from the School of Common Thought.

They think alike. Move alike. Resist alike. They're comfortable with their herd mentality. As a Soloist, you think differently, and what's more, you're often your own leader.

But you can't just ignore Sheeple. Fail to figure out how to deal with the masses, and they may trample you in their effort to stay in their ruts.

It's not that they can't think for themselves. They just won't. Work, bosses, and the daily grind have beaten them down. They've learned their lesson when it comes to taking chances or exploring untested pathways. Better to stay the course and keep on marching down that narrow, prescribed route. So what if little good ever comes of it? The Sheeple figures it really can't be all bad.

Rarely do we think of Sheeple as dangerous. But when they move, it's in one direction and as a solid, unstoppable force. Kind of like a glacier that takes coffee breaks. Changing their course, however slightly, is difficult. Unless you're ready to be a strong, clever Soloist, you may find yourself resigned to falling in step with the rest of the Sheeple – and there goes your career!

Since moving Sheeple en masse is so unwieldy, your best bet is to take them on one at a time. Separated from the crowd, their individual personalities begin to manifest and you can make some headway. Unfortunately, this takes time. But win an individual Sheeple over to your cause, and you may be pleasantly surprised. Once converted, a Sheeple sprouts into a devout evangelist, endowed with a gift for herding other Sheeple toward your cause.

Don't get cocky! Remember, the Sheeple mind-set is often only useful for one thing at a time. The converted Sheeple is far from autonomous. If he's been playing Sheeple for years, he isn't going to develop initiative overnight. Indeed, a little initiative for a Sheeple can be as dangerous as a little knowledge. He may blindly follow the last direction he received, trampling right over you.

Which brings us to how most people respond to Sheeple on an emotional level. "My reaction to Sheeple usually centers around yelling," says Shane Elliott, a senior rich-media architect for an international digital interactive advertising agency, who has worked with his share of Sheeple. Not surprisingly, barking at Sheeple is not advised. It usually results in scaring the Sheeple and causing them to stampede . . . to someone else who might be a bit more kind.

Meetings reinforce Sheeple behavior: aimless nodding, gentle grunts, and vacuous gazing. Everything but active participation. The effect is deadening, especially because all too often, the people you really need to hear from won't make a peep. "Often it's the group dynamic that overloads," says Pete Johnson of HP. He learned that one of his talented engineers would never talk about design at meetings. But walking with him back to their cubes, Johnson saw that the man often had enlightening ideas. Getting them out was the challenge. "He's the opposite of the Bulldozer," says Johnson of the Sheeple engineer. "He's the person who worries so much about what everybody thinks that he's scared." Johnson helped hold the man's hand during meetings. He'd say in front of the group, "Hey, Brian! The other day you were making that point to me in your cube . . ." By leading him along, Johnson was able to reassure the shy engineer and gradually get him to contribute in meetings.

Sheeple present unique challenges. But there can be an upside. While it can be tough to get their little hooves moving, Sheeple offer economies of scale. "Get one Sheeple to go with you, and you can get all of them to go," says international management consultant Bryan Mekechuk. Find the leader of the Sheeple – that man or woman with fluffier wool and shinier hooves. Then, as he says, "discover a way to make them feel special, some subtle motivation, and you can move the herd."

Try compliments in an e-mail or a group setting. Grant Sheeple higher status with cool titles or prime cube space. "They won't have a hot button; they're Sheeple," says Mekechuk. At the crack of five o'clock, they're gone. The trick is not to give them the hard stuff. Keep it simple. Lower your expectations: "Find the feather you need to tickle them with – you don't need a baseball bat."

COMBO PLATTERS

As you consider the Ten Least Wanted at your company, you will discover that some of the worst threats are the multiple offenders – men and women who combine two or more archetypes. For instance, Bob's a Switchblade and a Bulldozer. Not only does Bob excel at stabbing people in the back, but he enjoys mowing them down before storming on to his next victim.

There's the time-gobbling Minute Man known for his never-ending questions who suddenly one day is spewing answers like a Know-It-None and just won't stop. Or Nancy the Smiley Face/Stop Sign. She seems so nice. She even brings in cookies once a week. What's not to like? Sure, she throws up more red lights than the transportation department, but because she does it with a gleaming smile, it's going to take you months before you realize that she hates every single thing you've ever suggested.

Tangling with the Ten Least Wanted is a lifelong journey. As you rise up the ranks of your chosen profession, your skill in confronting the archetypes will help reduce your aggravation and increase your opportunities to become that more independent, resourceful person – the heart of our healthy People Hating philosophy and the subject of our next chapter, "The Soloist." You'll become more perceptive about who pushes your buttons, while removing the wiring that sets you off.

Yes, it all starts with good old-fashioned People Hating. Anyone can do that. But it takes a Soloist to effectively incorporate the Ten Least Wanted into how you get stuff done.

TWO

FLYING SOLO

5. The Soloist

Four decades ago, *Fortune* did a study of the most valued characteristics in an employee. The magazine found that teamwork was ranked tenth. Not first, second, or even fifth. Jump forward to 2005, and *Fortune*'s follow-up survey showed that teamwork had climbed to #1.

We live in the Age of Corporate Teamwork. CEOs, best-selling books, and business evangelists tout the central role of teamwork in everything from productivity to innovation. This cult began with American multinational firms imitating the quality and productivity methodology of top Japanese corporations. There was nothing wrong with this twentieth-century manufacturing marvel. Inspired in part by the brilliant author and consultant W. Edwards Deming, this movement helped build giants like Toyota and Sony.

But there has often been one element missing in the companies that have struggled to copy this modern industrial revolution: the human spark. In the forty years since *Fortune* did its original study, America has managed to abandon what had defined it for two centuries: ingenuity. Whatever happened to the rugged individualist? To the Theodore Roosevelts, Benjamin Franklins, and A. P. Gianninis?

Corporate America is in the midst of a crisis. The spirit of the individual has played a huge part in forging our nation's history. Yet the scourge of teamwork pap has made solo efforts in companies seem unwanted, crazy, even dangerous.

We have a solution: the Soloist.

A path for the rugged individual within you, a way to survive and thrive no matter how team-infested your company. No, we can't hope to reconfigure corporate dogma on teamwork, the current holiest of holies. But we can at least give you the weapons you need to succeed in spite of it.

The tools of the Soloist will give you a leg up in the critical battle against the Ten Least Wanted, whether it's the Bulldozer boss, the snarky Switchblade down the hall, or the Stop-Signing Spreadsheet in marketing. The Soloist sees them coming or has honed his skills to the point that he reacts on the fly.

There's pride and a new sense of self in becoming a Soloist. Instead of thinking of yourself as a staffer in a big company, the manager of a division, or a top executive, you begin to define yourself in concrete individualistic terms. You are a brand unto yourself. Brainstormer extraordinaire. Marketing whiz. Charismatic project leader. We're not suggesting that many companies don't value these skills; it's just that in the current climate of political correctness, the team *is* the new individual.

There's a reason why teamwork is so in vogue. We've all seen the corporate videos of fresh-scrubbed and suited executives, brainstorming around a conference table in some high-tech sterile room: Spewing out ideas on flip charts. Manipulating a fantastic holographic prototype in midair. Furiously building upon one another's concepts. All culminating in a rousing cheer of unbridled marketing glee.

In real life, however, talented people often become shackled by underperforming teams, slacker teammates, and out-of-the-loop bosses. Small wonder that Soloists hate people. The Soloist has unlocked the integral connection between concentrated individual effort and accomplishment. The smallest human interference at the wrong time can foul up a Soloist. Others innocently think they're only interrupting you for a minute or two. Some of these idiots even think they're giving you a much-needed break. But it's not the break you need. You were on course, and now you have to find the wind again.

There's a very subtle dynamic at play.

The Soloist is not a loner, a recluse, or a maverick. After all, you're not antisocial – you just hate people.

Think of a Soloist as a first-chair violinist. "The first-chair player of the first violin section . . . is called the 'concertmaster,' and has special responsibilities," says *The NPR Classical Music Companion.* "Playing the orchestral solos that are written for their instrument, setting the style and tone for their section, and leading their section by setting high standards of beauty, accuracy, and rhythmic reliability."

In other words, a Soloist fits smoothly within a group, playing with it expertly while often leading or accompanying fellow members. At the same time, the Soloist excels when he or she gets to perform alone, taking the Ensemble (more on this later) to new heights while demonstrating skills and talents that inspire.

The Soloist seeks a higher plane. Coming to terms with the types of people we all hate, the Soloist is better able to handle the week's flying crapfest – the jerk in the neighboring cube, the impossible customer, the maddening boss. Soloists separate people into two classes: those they hate, and those they can endure, like, and love. It's more than a skill, and it's more than an art. It's a discipline. By creatively channeling their natural frustration with troublesome people and situations, Soloists begin to craft a career and world where obstacles rarely blunt their progress. They become what used to be called unflappable.

The Soloist is keenly aware of the difference between creative, innovative effort and mind-numbing groupthink. By cutting loose from the pack whenever possible – physically or mentally – the Soloist reaches new levels of performance.

Today, the value of the group in corporations is assumed. Companies, universities, and society itself have long pummeled us with the idea that the team trumps the individual. But where's the proof?

Research dating back nearly a century suggests the opposite may be true – that as the team expands, individual productivity declines. In 1913, Maximilien Ringelmann, a French agricultural engineer, put the theory to the test with a physical, real-world experiment. He engineered a virtual tug-of-war that measured the difference between solo and mass effort. Ringelmann had individuals and groups pull on a rope connected to a strain gauge.

His experiment revealed that – surprise, surprise – even a century ago, there were slackers: the average cog in the group of eight yanked just half as hard as the average individual tugging that rope all by his lonesome. Even with a trio, individual performance sagged by nearly 20 percent.

The results suggested an unexpected challenge to conventional wisdom: the more people you throw at a problem, the less each contributes.

Ringelmann chalked up this decrease in performance to losses from coordination and "social loafing" – the concept that people in groups decrease their individual effort. Today, it's called the Ringelmann effect.

More recent research has shown that "motivational losses" may also contribute to the decline. Elite women rowers in an eight, for instance, have been clearly shown to row less vigorously together than they do as individuals. Researchers chalk up this form of social loafing to the duration of the task – the longer the group rows, the more performance suffers. There's an intangible factor. When the team's moody, they don't pull.

But it isn't only the debilitating Ringelmann effect that brings many people down when working in corporations.

David Johnson, our psychologist, says that one challenge Soloists face in larger companies is that many people are at cross-purposes: "A lot of people seek work in larger organizations because they're looking for friendships and relationships. They like to be there. They like to chat and collaborate and work with other people."

It may be the most critical conflict of interest you'll face in your career.

Sometimes those friendship-seeking office folk, Johnson says, don't always put the job first. "Their focus is on being with you, not realizing that's exactly what you find annoying," he says. "You just want to get the job done."

Science, product innovation, and history are on the side of the Soloist. Business is full of inspiring stories about individuals who earned fame and fortune through hard work

Great Soloists in History: A. P. Giannini

Thrown from his San Francisco bed by the Great Quake of 1906, Amadeo Giannini (the son of Italian immigrants) didn't panic as the city burned. He hitched a team of horses to a produce wagon he'd borrowed and raced into town to the rubble that had been the Bank of Italy, which he'd founded two years before. Sifting through the remains, he salvaged and then quickly loaded $2 million in gold, coins, and securities into the wagon, covering it over with vegetables. In the days that followed, Giannini set up shop in the city's North Beach area by plunking a wooden plank across two barrels and, from there, extending credit to needy businesses and individuals. He went on to found the Bank of America.

and ambition. Breakthroughs have often come from a lone genius or two toiling in the dark. Consider Alexander Graham Bell, and William Hewlett and David Packard, and the Google guys. One or a few Soloists striking an initial spark were behind nearly every enterprising company or innovation. Today, even the individual products or services that continue companies' leadership often owe their incubation to less than a handful of renegade Soloists – from iRobot's Looj and the classic 3M Post-it, to some of our top technology breakthroughs.

Consider Apple's iPod. Back at the turn of the century, it seemed everybody was rolling out another MP3 player – and nobody cared. It was going to take something novel to grab the public's attention. Hello, Tony Fadell. The entrepreneurial cofounder and CTO of Philips's Mobile Computing

Group went on to launch Fuse, his own firm, in the late nineties, targeting consumer electronics. Fadell was aiming for a small, hard-drive-based music player combined with a Napster-style music subscription service. Fuse failed to get a second round of financing, and when it closed up shop, Fadell started shopping his music maker around Silicon Valley. After six weeks at RealNetworks, he reportedly butted heads with CEO Rob Glaser. Fadell took his ball, but rather than go home, he skipped on to Apple.

History depends on who's doing the telling at this point. In early 2001, Steve Jobs was either smitten by Fadell's concept or else had a similar product up his sleeve. He drafted the Soloist Fadell into the Apple nest and supplied him with a thirty-person team of designers, programmers, and hardware engineers. He also handed him a deadline: have a product ready in time for Christmas sales. Sure enough, the first iPod rolled out in October, and not even the commerce-halting events of 9/11 could dim the rush by the personal-music crowd.

Fadell's story demonstrates the importance of Soloists in driving corporate innovation and the uneasy response that some CEOs have to their role. The tamed entrepreneur is now comfortably chained to the nest with the title of senior VP of the iPod division. Apple downplays Fadell's unofficial "Father of the iPod" moniker, which floats around the Web, and requests for interviews are routinely denied by the company.

Conflicts over credit for ground-breaking corporate work are nothing new. It's one of the reasons that Soloists in large companies tend to be so unsung. Yes, companies depend on their innovative ideas and maverick spirit, but once they hit the ball out of the park, the organization often decides that the world should only see the figurehead who waves the company flag, in this case the legendary Steve Jobs. Real-life stories of Soloists are nearly always about overcoming inertia and organizational obstacles.

The story line of a successful Soloist often features the traditional hurdles: skeptical superiors, corporate dogma that often seems bent on thwarting independent innovation, and then the winning breakthrough – the corporate version of the Hollywood ending. Ken Kutaragi of Sony, for instance, came up with a hot idea by watching his daughter play an early game made by another company: Nintendo. He thought the sound sucked – and as an audio engineer, he decided to do something about it. Kutaragi started tinkering on the side, developing an impressive digital chip for the next-generation Nintendo game, the SPC7000. When his bosses learned of his on-the-job hobby, he was nearly fired. But fortunately, Sony's CEO realized that Kutaragi was onto something and encouraged him to go full bore on developing a full-fledged CD-ROM-based Nintendo. When Nintendo passed on the technology, Kutaragi led Sony's efforts in what became an international hit: the PlayStation.

Kutaragi rose to the head of Sony's Computer Entertainment division, one of many examples of Soloists who didn't ask permission, wouldn't take no for an answer, and went on to carve out impressive careers.

More than history is on the side of the Soloist. Turns out a classic saying that dates back to medieval times, "Out of sight, out of mind," applies to your coworkers. The science is in, and it says that teams often distract us from all sorts of work and tasks. Human physiology suggests that the mere sight of another coworker may be bad for business. The latest research, conducted at the University of Calgary and published in the journal *Human Movement Science,* demonstrates that people in your work environment are slowing you down.

The study involved individuals working on a computer task alone or with a partner tackling a different but related task in full view. Just the sight of another person working slowed individual progress. When the partner left the room, however, the effect vanished.

Why the drag on performance? It's not unlike runners in a race who spin their heads around to watch competitors nipping at their heels, losing precious seconds.

The reason this visual stimulus can be so distracting is because of what researchers call our mirror neuron system. "Humans have a response-interpretation mechanism hardwired into their central nervous system," Dr. Tim Welsh, the study's lead researcher, told sciencedaily.com. It's a phenomenon that makes us mimic what someone in our field of vision is doing, even if it has nothing to do with the task you're focusing on.

Welsh's radical conclusion: working all by your lonesome may increase productivity.

Few companies will have the insight to implement Welsh's plan anytime soon. But taking the Soloist path provides a kind of virtual isolation. You're still sitting at your desk. And yes, office mates are likely in sight. But now they pose fewer risks. The Soloist is less likely to be distracted during a deadline crunch by such annoyances. He stays on task by separating himself from the hectic workplace when necessary. He recognizes the critical difference between business and busyness.

Perhaps the best reason for becoming a Soloist is to make the most of something you can't plan on. Inspiration.

When your business day is crammed with meetings, phone calls, e-mails, and the multitude of human interruptions, Inspiration must wait its turn. Which is exactly what Inspiration doesn't do. It strikes suddenly, and usually when you least expect it.

The Soloist is always ready for Inspiration.

This is not the routine in most companies. Schedules and agendas rule. Meetings and deadlines cannot wait. Phone calls and e-mails need to be answered. We often find ourselves spinning like a break-dancer among the tasks that crowd our calendar. The idea that you would dare miss a meeting because you were pursuing a great idea would be sacrilege in most companies. Imagine making the team wait because you were having a breakthrough. Imagine a manager who recognized that your ideas might be more valuable than your physical presence. Imagine others being inspired by a Soloist's inspiration.

Yes, you're getting close to understanding the world of a Soloist. A world where you take the time and make the space to invite ideas to stay awhile and visit. Where you can play with them, expand them, and make them come to life.

Some offices are more "Soloist friendly" than others. Jen Klise is one of those lucky corporate warriors who gets paid to be a Soloist. As a group manager at Target headquarters in Minneapolis, she leads seven staffers whose collective goal is to come up with three to five home-run products every year. At any one time, Klise is working on ten to fifteen projects at various stages of development. But during the inspiration phase, when she's looking at customer insights, trends, and demographics to home in on what she hopes will be a bull's-eye, she usually goes it alone – often for weeks or months at a time. "We all have our own projects. When we're operating as Soloists, we try to incubate them to the point where they become real or not," says Klise. "This is often best done as an individual because you can have a vision for competitive advantage."

The trouble with trying to do this early-stage innovation from a team perspective is that the initiative and imagination can flounder. As Klise notes, "It's often difficult to communicate that vision in just a business plan."

Becoming a Soloist is not something others can do for you. Not a friend, partner, or coworker. The Soloist comes from within. It's not a formula or a rule book or a series of exercises. Your ability as a Soloist is directly related to your willingness to embrace the fundamentals.

The Six Soloist Principles

- ▶ Separation from the pack is not rejection of the pack.
- ▶ Achievement won't always make me popular.
- ▶ Change is easy; anticipating change hurts.
- ▶ Creativity doesn't fit on a spreadsheet.
- ▶ Genius does not punch a clock.
- ▶ I matter.

Once you begin to make these principles foremost in your mind throughout the workday, the Path of the Soloist becomes clear. And by believing in your individual potential and powers of creativity, you will become more creative.

This isn't just wishful thinking by a couple of People Haters. A recent study conducted by professor Barry Staw of the Haas School of Business and by Cornell University's

Jack Goncalo demonstrates that believing in your individual ability and uniqueness may lead to more innovative ideas.

It's mind over mediocre: believe that you're a Soloist, and you will become more innovative.

The professors divided two hundred business students into two kinds of groups. One group answered questions that encouraged them to be more individualistic: "Why do you think you are not like most other people?" or "Why do you think it might be advantageous to 'stand out'?"

Conversely, they asked other groups to answer questions that encouraged them to adopt behavior that the professors term more grouplike or collectivistic: "Why do you think you are like most other people?" or "Why do you think it might be advantageous to 'blend in' with other people?"

The idea was simple: the study was priming the students to think either as individuals or as a group.

Both groups were asked to brainstorm on a business challenge. A university-run restaurant had gone bust. The school administration was struggling. It was up to the students to dream up new ideas for a business to take the restaurant's place.

The results were revealing. By every measure, the groups primed to be more individualistic were more innovative, coming up with novel ideas, such as a library or a café with live music and free massages. In contrast, the group-thinkers tended to spit out same-old ideas, such as another restaurant.

The individualistic groups did more than come up with lots of innovative ideas. Their productivity increased: they generated more ideas. The lesson here is that there is a central creative power in individuals and group members who believe that they are individuals:

"On every measure, individualistic groups were more creative than collectivistic groups when instructed to do so," wrote the professors. "When creativity is explicitly desired, individualism will serve to facilitate such performance."

Deviant ideas, they wrote, are the heart of innovation, and individualistic groups tend to lack manners and "be divisive and even unruly."

We applaud the individualism demonstrated by these two Soloist professors. Their bold work contradicts many recent business best sellers and much of the academic research of the past two decades. They also had the guts to declare that turning individuals into groupthinkers is dangerous. Once programmed as a groupthinker, one may not find it so easy to shake free. The study showed no support for the notion that collectivistic groups can act creatively if they are simply instructed to do so. Just think what the cumulative effect might be of putting in a twenty-year collectivistic prison sentence at a *Fortune* 500 company.

The Soloist Flavors

Soloists tend to fall into one of four basic categories.

▶ **The Stay-Put**

   Treats his company position as a nest, and finds creative ways to forage during the day and build nests for other budding Soloists. Stay-Puts are often found working inside companies under interesting titles like director of innovation and vice president of creativity.

▶ **The Nest Hopper**

   Builds a nice nest at one corporation, but still isn't allowed the freedom he needs. He moves over to a company that grants him more room to build out his dream nest. It's the deal he can't refuse. It's about authority, independence, starting something. Though the Nest Hopper might jump to another large company, he'll often find less bureaucracy and supervision with more freedom in a smaller company where he can truly be himself.

► **The Serial Soloist**
Juggles a range of work partners and projects. Some are collaborations and some are individual efforts. The Serial Soloist may connect with multiple partners and also break away for several hours of solo time.

► **The Super Soloist**
Yearns to move on. Sooner or later, the Super Soloist is compelled to leave the nest altogether to join, or more often start, a new enterprise.

Chance and opportunity often influence what sort of Soloist you become. Early in your career, you may consider yourself a Nest Hopper or Serial Soloist.

You might view the corporate world as Debbie Vargo did twenty years ago. Vargo had gone to college in California and came to P&G on what she called the two-year plan. "I could not imagine living my whole life in the Midwest," she says. "I'd work there two years, then we'd move to California and I'd join another company."

Fate intervened. While on a business trip in San Francisco, the pregnant Vargo went into premature labor. Her baby's heart rate dropped precipitously, and she had to have an emergency C-section. Dylan survived, but the tiny infant was losing weight fast and could only breathe with a respirator. As Vargo recalls, the insurance company "didn't know what to do with us" and only cared about what Dylan's care cost. The insurance company wanted to hospitalize her baby for months in California – thousands of miles from Vargo's friends and family in Cincinnati.

But P&G stepped in, acting boldly on behalf of its young Soloist. The company paid for Stanford's air ambulance to fly Vargo, her husband, and infant Dylan back to Ohio. Two doctors and a nurse in a Learjet, at a cost of about $20,000.

Dylan not only survived – he thrived. He's now a six-foot-tall, 180-pound young man heading off to college. "That intervention showed how much the company cared about me as a person," says Vargo. "When you think about bonding, that's really bonding to a human."

Despite her dreams of California and thoughts of working for several other companies throughout her career, Vargo never left P&G. "That made a difference to my stay-putness," she says. " I had no doubt at that point. That was my defining moment."

Today, Vargo is a twenty-six-year veteran of P&G. She's the director of PŪR, the company's water-filtration division, and heads up a group of forty individuals and Ensembles. As we'll learn in our next chapter, she's passionate about her job and has no plans to leave anytime soon.

Target's Jen Klise, whom we just met, joined the retail giant right out of college and put in eleven straight years. Wanting to spend more time with her family, she decided to quit and try consulting. Part of the appeal was that she'd be able to take it easy, but then her business grew and so did her expertise. "I had only known Target, but working with Coke, GM, and General Mills, I began to see things differently." By exploring a wide range of companies, Klise learned that "some of the smartest people in companies are middle level." We might add that they're also the people who do the bulk of the creative work: the Soloists.

After two years spent exploring the outside world, Klise and her business partner were recruited to rejoin Target with greater opportunities and rewards. The irony isn't lost on her. By having the courage to leave the nest, she found more opportunities with her longtime original employer, Target, for which she's been happily employed – for the second time – for the past four years.

DIVERGENT THINKING

One of today's problems within work groups is that everyone knows what everyone else is working on. The team that's trying to design a new baby stroller has everyone working on the obvious goal: a better baby stroller. The limit of that approach is that the majority of the ideas are nearly always derivative: modifications of existing products, knockoffs of competitors' products, or throwbacks to simpler designs. The current method of ideation practiced by the world's top design firms is to find inspiration from tangents. For instance, if a cool new baby stroller is the goal, exploration might be done in the area of hot sports cars, motorcycles, and skateboards. That's a strong first step, but even so, the designers often remain anchored to the baby-stroller target, preventing them from stepping more fully (and creatively) in other directions.

That inertia is why none of the established baby-stroller manufacturers came up with any major innovations since the device was originally introduced in 1733. Enter divergent thinking. The breakthrough here came from a total outsider, Phil Baechler, a newspaperman with zero knowledge of mechanical design, let alone baby strollers. In the early eighties, Baechler, a devout jogger, wanted to spend more time with his infant son but found that the existing strollers weren't up to the task. Inspired by mountain bikes, Baechler launched the Baby Jogger in 1984: three large bicycle-style wheels, a superior suspension system, and a big canopy to protect the child from the elements. It quickly became the must-have stroller for the parent on the go.

That's great. But how can a Soloist within a company stimulate this kind of imaginative development? One way is to be the only one who knows the true target of the assignment. For example, we begin with explorations that spin off the core idea. In one case, Christopher Ranch, the food-products company, brought us in to name a new specialty garlic. We went to the grocery store to see the wrong way to brand produce. Then we cooked up a few secret assignments for our team. No one had any idea what the real project was all about. Some team members were told the client was a new Italian-bistro chain. Another learned that a statue, a female counterpart to Michelangelo's *David,* had been unearthed, and she needed a name. A third assignment was to name a wine being produced as a joint venture between Mondavi and automaker Ferrari. These Divergent Thinking exercises helped us carve an original path to the ultimate brand: Monviso, a mountain in the Italian Alps in the same region where the garlic was originally harvested.

The lesson? What seem from the outside to be roundabout approaches to projects can spur innovation and deliver superior results.

FINDING YOUR SOLOIST ROOTS

Over the course of your career, you may embody the different types of Soloist – everything from a Nest Hopper to a Super Soloist. It all depends on the companies you're with and your particular needs and goals. A big motivating factor can be the people you're forced to put up with in the course of doing your job.

Every Soloist can trace back his history through the companies and experiences that helped give him the strength and independence to strike out on his own. We look at the successful people, entrepreneurs, and top executives within corporations, and somehow we often forget that they are human, forged by very unique circumstances. Consider Marc van Gerven, the GE veteran who went on to become an executive at Solaris, a promising solar-power startup. He was not quite a founder, but he was the fifth man in – not bad for a venture with $77 million in funding. The beauty of that, he says, was that as the company's first marketing and sales person, "you have to do it yourself."

How did he jump-start his efforts? Two weeks into the job, he met someone at a conference who worked for a giant solar-cell manufacturer. Strangely, not a single one of the world's top photovoltaic cell makers had invested in a solar startup.

Van Gerven was looking for just such a partner. He made his pitch. He got an appointment with the German company Q-Cells. It helped that he spoke fluent German. Van Gerven was ushered into a room full of people at Q-Cells' Thalheim office. The head of business development was blunt.

"Why am I talking to you?" was the first thing out of his mouth. "We get these requests every day."

As a Soloist, van Gerven didn't have to take the time to consult with a team or stall while he tried to reconfigure his presentation for this guy. He got right to it: "I was able to say in one sentence what his problem was. 'You need a more diversified product offering, and we've got it.'"

The executive got the point, and within eight months the firm made its first investment in Solaris, giving van Gerven and the company instant marketing credibility. Ten months later, Q-Cells poured in more cash. Though van Gerven now has a modest staff, he says, "I have a team outside the company. Friends in the industry." Q-Cells recently became the world's largest solar-cell manufacturer.

Where do you cut your Soloist teeth? Van Gerven refined his Soloist personality while working against the grain of corporate homogenization, at giant multinationals like Unocal and General Electric. Years of working in the rough-and-tumble oil and gas business taught him to connect the dots from complex sources and distill it down into what he calls "a picture of something that matters."

By the time he had put in his time at Unocal and the software firm Autodesk, and begun finding his way at the organizational labyrinth that is GE, van Gerven had developed his own formula for Solocrafting. We've integrated it with our own research.

Solocrafting in Four Easy Steps

1. Stop Talking

If you talk about it, nothing gets done.

2. Start Doing

Just start doing the project.

3. Stop Asking
If you ask for a dedicated team (or resources), you're not getting it done.

4. Make Them Believe
Make people believe you can get it done, and they'll come help whether they report to you or not.

Simplicity goes a long way for the Soloist. The bigger the company, the more entangled the bureaucracy. "If you can't explain in one sentence what you're doing, then you need the bureaucracy and everything else," says van Gerven.

The firm assigned him a mentor, as it does to many employees. Van Gerven learned to reach out to his mentor and to the head of the oil and gas division, who eventually became a supporter. "People started to request my services," says van Gerven. "I branched out to do different things in GE that were not part of my team."

It's a story we encountered over and over in our interviews and research. By taking the initiative to explore tangents outside of his core responsibilities, the Soloist builds his expertise and strength. First coworkers, then superiors, and finally the company at large comes to rely on his Soloist skills, which continue to grow and branch out into other areas.

Perhaps you lack Marc van Gerven's confidence or people skills. Maybe you're pretty good at your job but not so hot at office politics. You're not exactly sure why, but you may even rub people the wrong way. Here's the good news: you may never win a popularity contest, but the freedom and happiness of a Soloist is within your grasp.

Consider the remarkable tale of Craig Newmark, founder of Craigslist (www.craigslist.org), the world's largest Internet classified pages, where you can find everything from a new bicycle to a girlfriend and an apartment for both of them. We spoke to Newmark at length one afternoon and consider him proof of concept.

Newmark kicked off his programming career with IBM in its Boca Raton office, then spent nearly ten years in Detroit and the last couple in Pittsburgh. Newmark considered many of his years as a programmer pretty good, but by the end, not so good. He was stuck in a marketing branch office. For a technical man like Newmark, it was a bad fit. "I lived la vida Dilbert," he confessed to us. "Sometimes I would alienate people. It didn't matter if I was right. I was clumsy."

Fortune struck. By 1993, IBM had hit a rough spot. As Newmark put it, "The company was kind of panicky. That wasn't pleasant." Like a lot of folks, Newmark believed in the giant multinational corporation that had been his lifeblood for nearly two decades. Why would he do anything else in his life? He was a skilled programmer – a full-on nerd – but IBM had thousands who fit that category. "I kept hanging on, thinking things would be better, that someone as technical as me would find an opportunity. I was wrong."

How easily that might have been the short, sad tale of another unfulfilled corporate cog.

It was an age when the marketing wonks at IBM resented the geeks. Newmark realized he wasn't going to be happy. He sought out new opportunities in California. He boldly lined up interviews and landed a meeting at Charles Schwab. He got the job and excelled at the giant financial firm but found new problems. "The atmosphere was very political," he recalls. "Infighting was more important than getting things done." Newmark noticed how the company seldom gave credit to the guys who actually did the work.

That was one of the things that bugged Newmark about big companies: not sharing. Then Newmark got lucky. "Schwab had a bit of an implosion, and I decided to take a buyout and try freelancing." Surprisingly, fellow workers at Schwab had told Newmark he'd earn more and find better opportunities by striking out on his own. Newmark says he made a misstep or two along the way, but then won some plum contract jobs, among them helping Bank of America develop its home banking. Like a lot of geeks, he thought that Internet thing was cool. He dug the giving part of it. "I thought I should give back a little myself. I listened more and decided to start a simple CC list."

He can only guess at his official launch: around March of 1995. Craig Newmark began Craigslist, a crude list of people wanting to sell stuff – furniture, bikes, apartments – not to mention that other feature of the newspaper classified, men looking for women, women looking for men, men looking for women *and* men . . . He had no intention of building a business. "It was just something I did. It felt good. I was connecting with people."

Craigslist was not an instant failure – or hit: "It was very slow. Gradual." Still, within a few months, someone told Newmark that he had accidentally built a brand. Two years after Newmark began his hobby, he passed some milestones. First, he received about a million pageviews a month. Then Microsoft wanted him to run its banner ads. Newmark thought it over. "I felt I was already paid more than I needed as a contract programmer," he recalls. "I do regard banner ads as frequently annoying."

And so, Craig Newmark, bless his heart, said no to Microsoft.

By 1998, Newmark reached that make-or-break point

for the successful Soloist. Though he was running the operation out of his modest San Francisco home, Craigslist was growing so fast that he needed lots of help. He tried turning over his hobby to volunteers. "Someone needed to assert leadership," he says frankly. "I didn't. As a manager I kind of suck."

Newmark admits that it wasn't easy, but he was finally talked into turning his hobby into a real company – incorporating, hiring a manager and staff. Today, it's still nearly run like a nonprofit. Listings are free, except those for jobs and real estate. Experts estimate 2008 earnings at $80 million, with an eye-popping ten billion pageviews a month. Henry Blodget ranks Craigslist as one of the world's top twenty-five most valuable start-ups, and postulates that if Newmark ever wanted to sell the darn thing "we're conservatively looking at a business worth $5 billion."

This from a hobby. A geek who could have easily remained an anonymous programmer the rest of his life. Newmark exhibits no visible profit motive. The notion, as he says, "that we've helped out millions, maybe tens of millions, of people" appears to give him the most pleasure. "It is a service."

If not for IBM hitting a rocky spot in the early nineties, Newmark might never have discovered his Soloist gene. "I'd say people need to listen to their instincts," he says. "If they're not happy, they need to look elsewhere." Newmark says that he was in denial for a long time at IBM, and probably should have gotten out six years before he did.

Like a lot of Soloists who have written their own ticket, Craig can do his own thing now. He remains an unapologetic nerd. Unlike some entrepreneurs, he shows no compulsion to start a second or third new company. He comes across as a character out of a Dilbert cartoon who figured out how to play the game despite, or perhaps because of, himself.

Soloists, as we've noted, come in all flavors. Serial Soloists are one of the highest levels of the discipline. They've got lots of plates spinning. Not everyone wants or needs this level of activity, but if you're wondering how to pull off one sideline at a time, there's a lot to learn from someone capable of juggling many.

The Serial Soloist has passions to spare. Rather than limit himself to a single extra pursuit, a clever Soloist will devise a way to pursue several simultaneously. Shane Elliott is a consummate Serial Soloist who manages to be one with wit, humor, and charm. He's the Sheeple-hating Web designer we met earlier. Though Elliott is in Los Angeles, he's connected by phone, IM, and e-mail to offices in San Francisco, New York, Austin, Seattle, and London. He's a busy guy, logging nearly fifty hours a week.

This might not sound like much to corporate soldiers who routinely put in more than sixty. But Elliott is also an actor. This is nothing unusual when you live close to Hollywood. Except Elliott is a *working* actor. You've seen his face in commercials for Twix, Bud Light, Toyota, Honda, and T.G.I. Friday's. And those are just the spots he *got*. Multiply those by a factor of a hundred to account for the endless string of auditions, callbacks, and second callbacks. During regular business hours.

Elliott's third gig is as director and executive producer of *Fries on the Side,* a live sketch-comedy group that's been playing once a week for six years. It's something like producing a homegrown version of *Saturday Night Live.*

Clearly, Elliott's a Soloist who's figured out how to work it. Part of his secret is that he's good enough at his day job to have dictated his job terms. When Elliott took his latest position, he was offered plenty of money. But he needed something more to fully engage his Soloist skills. He asked for – and got – the freedom to work two days a week outside of the office. He wanted the time and space to make his auditions, dream up his sketches, and, yes, get his regular work done.

Of course, Soloists need not be actors or artists. Nor must their companies or line of work be considered exciting. It's how they balance their individual wants with those of the company. Take Amabel Garcia, the learning solutions specialist for AAA we met earlier, who heads up project teams at the San Francisco headquarters – even though she lives 570 miles away, in Las Vegas. Her family lives in Nevada, and she definitely isn't moving to San Francisco. There was a learning curve in working with people hundreds of miles away, but she knew if her supervisor was willing to work with her, she could pull off the long-distance job. Her method: "I stay in touch with my team with IM all day, so I'm always in contact." In the morning she IMs her teammates on a project, tells them what work she's completed, where they can find it on the server, what she's going to tackle next – and when she'll be done.

Ironically, it's more communication than she'd ever have if everyone were in the same room – in one another's faces.

Before she eats lunch, she'll let everyone know how much progress she's made. Garcia also phones her team members, collectively or individually, two or three times a day. Then there's the hundred e-mails a day. And it's not as if she never gets face time with the people she leads. She flies to San Francisco monthly to meet with her team for two to five days.

What's more, Garcia juggles these roles by working in relative physical isolation. Once or twice a week, she works from her home office. The rest of the week, she's cubing it at the nearest equivalent to a company office: AAA's call center in Las Vegas. It's packed with people taking non-stop calls from auto-club clients. Garcia's cube is in a vast space, totally apart from the call center. "Other than when I go to the break room and say 'Hi,' I don't interact with the call people," she says.

Far from complaining of loneliness, Garcia enjoys her setup.

Unique problems do crop up when you're so far from the action. Things that fall through the cracks because you're not physically present. Occasions when you know what that person needs to do – and he doesn't – because you are not working side by side.

Garcia is finding that IMing and remotely collaborating through Google Docs – skills that she and her Ensemble are rapidly developing – help bridge that physical gap.

Garcia and Elliott demonstrate that just about anybody has the potential to bring the Way of the Soloist to his or her job. Take a look around and see where opportunities might already exist. In the following chapter, Solocrafting, we'll show you how to take advantage of opportunities you never knew existed.

A NEW KIND OF REBEL

The Soloist works on his own terms. While adhering to basic office rules and workload, he fashions a new personal work environment that stretches beyond the office. The Soloist takes time every day to break free of the electronic chains of e-mail, cell, and text. He braves the risk of personalizing his cube, office, or workspace. He makes it a place that is comfortable to work in – as opposed to a place that work is comfortable with.

The Soloist is a rebel without being a revolutionary.

It's your cause. Whether or not others rally to the call isn't really your thing. You took the test; you know the truth. You hate people.

Some of them may want to follow your lead and take up their own causes. That's up to them. They'll make good allies if and when you choose to create a small team of Soloists – what we call an Ensemble.

CREATING YOUR ENSEMBLE

Ensemble is a French word. We're interested in its musical definition: "The united performance of an entire group of singers, musicians, etc." When we then apply the term "ensemble" to work, we're not talking about a typical project team or work group. Ensembles, instead, tend to be under the radar. Unauthorized. Unbudgeted. Not that they aren't absolutely essential. They're helping you get your job done – often in a way that the official forms and channels can't.

The members of your Ensemble may change depending on the needs of the project. Bear in mind their individual strengths and weaknesses. Think more in terms of a duo or quartet than a football squad.

Four Steps to Starting Your Ensemble
1. Just do it.
You don't need to reveal the identities of your Ensemble members to anyone, nor that you even have

an Ensemble. Give other Soloists a reason to join: a great new product idea, marketing strategy, et cetera. Meet them outside the office whenever possible. Treat this like your secret club.

2. **Inspiration matters more than time.**
   Members of your Ensemble are talented. Busy. So don't be a jerk. Don't become one more annoyance. Quality, not quantity, is what counts here.

3. **These are people we do not hate.**
   It's a balancing act. Fail to give your Ensemble members the space and time apart they need, and it can all come crashing down. If it starts to smell like a project group, listen to your nose. Back off, or you risk losing them – and yourself.

4. **Nothing is forever, including your Ensemble.**
   Every Ensemble has a life span. When the task or project is completed, some Ensembles may die. Others may morph, blending with other members more suited to taking on a different goal.

It's important to keep in mind that an Ensemble starts with the inspiration of one or two Soloists. Don't confuse an Ensemble with a Skunk Works, the term often employed to describe large independent research and product efforts within an even larger company. Part of the lore of the worlds of high technology and aviation, the practice traces its history to the original Lockheed Martin Skunk Works, launched in the 1940s to speedily design and build generations of radical new aircraft like the stealth bomber. Skunk Works have had mixed results. They're big teams that often become unwieldy. They're sometimes too closely aligned to the parent company to create breakout solutions. And they can go wildly off target and produce nothing of value.

Ensembles have many advantages over Skunk Works–style innovation. An Ensemble derives its strength from the Soloist who brings it together and benefits from its collective force. You can pull together an Ensemble even if you're not heading a top project within Google or Boeing. You might be a midlevel manager or a young staffer with an eye to rising up the ladder. Or maybe just a hardy grunt who thrives on his time alone.

Perhaps the most easily identifiable Soloists are project leaders. When companies formally recognize big-time Soloists, they often reward them with a plum project and a nifty place to work, and tell them to come back in a few months or a year with a home run.

A number of Soloists end up leaving larger corporations in favor of smaller, more nimble companies. More often, Soloists are not looking to change jobs so much as they are seeking greater personal freedom in their current position – a freedom that grants them the opportunity to be more productive.

As vice president of new business at Procter & Gamble Health Care, Karl Ronn oversees a staff of six hundred. His managerial responsibilities are too large for him to be the Soloist who comes up with hot new products. Instead, he says that a huge part of his job has to do with inspiration: supporting the dreams of other Soloists and their Ensembles within the consumer-products giant. "A lot of the role I'll play with my Ensembles is that I'll try to get passionate about what they're getting passionate about. New products have to say something; they have to have a

Breaking the Four-Minute Mile

Roger Bannister is famous for being the first runner to break the four-minute mile, a record that had long been considered beyond the reach of man. But the secret is that he didn't do it alone. Bannister was a Soloist who carefully cultivated his Ensemble.

Two other runners seemed likely to beat England's Bannister to the goal. Australian John Landy had the most relentless training, while American Wes Santee had the greatest natural speed.

Bannister was gifted but had little time. He was making his rounds as a medical student soon to become a doctor. Landy had hours a day to train and Santee was a college student with two-hour practices. Bannister had to hop to his training, catching a train on his lunch hour and sneaking in thirty-five minutes at a shoddy track. His limited time made him more focused. In his lab work, he studied endurance and exercise, and then applied some of his findings to his training.

Bannister brought together his Ensemble: two friends to help him tackle the record. Sharing the pain and loneliness of training, they forged a plan. One would set the pace for Bannister on the fated day for the first two laps. The other for the third lap and as much as he could stomach of the last. Everything looked perfect until a few weeks before the planned record-breaking attempt. They hit the wall. They couldn't crack sixty-one seconds in their pivotal quarter-mile intervals. The pressure on Bannister was intense, and he was at a loss. Nothing they did made them any faster. So they tried something ludicrous.

The Soloist and his Ensemble took off for the Scottish Highlands to scale some heights. For three days they rock-climbed — something completely different from running. It was risky. One of Bannister's friends fell twenty-five feet and was only saved by the rope. They returned to Oxford with blisters and sore muscles, but thoroughly refreshed and exhilarated. When he stepped back on the track, Bannister averaged fifty-nine seconds a lap — a full two seconds faster than before he took his Ensemble excursion. Two weeks later, on May 6, 1954, Roger Bannister ran 3:59.4; he was the world's first to break the four-minute mile.

point of view," says Ronn, who, despite an intense work schedule, finds time to head up the marketing committee for the respected Cincinnati Symphony Orchestra, where he's had the rare experience of assisting a real conductor, the internationally famous, Grammy Award–winning Paavo Järvi. "What I like about Paavo is I get to sit down and talk to him about his vision. If the conductor does not bring a point of view, then the symphony is not worth playing. That applies to the conductor, the Ensemble, and the Soloist."

The best Ensembles have passion and a point of view, and draw talent like magnets. Jim Lynch was cleaning the gutters of his Massachusetts home one weekend when he stumbled onto a killer *business opp*. His day job was as an electrical engineer for iRobot. This was the ideal task for a robot, he told BNET, "because it fit into our company's three criteria: dumb, dirty, and dangerous." He worked up a quick prototype, made a presentation during a company "idea bake-off," and found himself green-lighted with a five-person team.

But Lynch never would have made the crazy deadline the company set for Looj the robot to hit the market if not for his reputation within the company as someone who leads cool projects. People walked up to him and volunteered to work on his gutter-cleaning robot. And that's not all. When Lynch realized he was over his head on the management side, he cleverly turned two of his more experienced peers into unofficial mentors.

Lynch was assembling his Ensemble on the fly – from the bottom and the top. Sometimes it happens even more organically. The good Soloist may not even realize he's part of an Ensemble. That may be the best kind of Ensemble of all.

An Ensemble doesn't have to be made up of other Soloists. If someone completing a single task will help you complete a project, engage him as long as you need to and then move on. And don't forget a more basic truth. Many members of your various Ensembles may come from outside your direct work environment – other divisions, branches – and even beyond your industry.

Sadly, many companies have created barriers to Ensembles. Resourcing, they call it. Formally the domain of lawyers, resourcing means that an employee has to log everything he does and indicate which minutes apply to which clients, all so the Spreadsheets can make sure to itemize, clock, and bill every second. "Is it billable?" is the question many professionals told us they get asked when they're trying to get some feedback from a teammate on a project. It's a constraint that an ambitious Soloist must find ways around.

Larger corporations often make an additional mistake: formalizing teamwork to the point that there's little room for the Ensemble style of collaboration. But we're encouraged that slowly but surely there is a growing recognition that big isn't necessarily better.

Software firms, in particular, burned by the sloppy and uncreative code that tends to be chunked out by massive programmer teams, are increasingly slimming down. There's a fresh recognition that much smaller teams – just three to six people – tend to be more successful. Jennifer Mueller, a professor of management at Wharton who has studied declining returns in larger corporate teams, says, "After about five people, there are diminishing returns on how much people will pull." This recalls the Ringelmann effect we discussed earlier.

We think there's evidence to suggest that three may be the magic number for an Ensemble. In classic studies of letters to number coding problems, trios seem to be the most effective. One recent University of Illinois study showed no improvement as group size increased from three to four to five. The authors suggested that coordination inefficiencies and "production blocking," the tendency of one person to shut out the ideas of others in a brainstorm or other group situation, might increase with greater numbers of participants.

As fans of European football, otherwise known as soccer, we note that even on a team of eleven players, the most creative and game-breaking plays are nearly always the result of the inspiring forays of two or three athletes – the power of an Ensemble. And the team with the best Ensemble often wins.

This analogy translates well to larger corporations. Some Soloists, stuck working in larger teams, draft an Ensemble from the team itself, focusing on working with just a few people, all of whom are very familiar with their tasks and goals.

We believe three to five is a good range for your Ensemble. As a Soloist, you may find it a question of preferences and style. Some like to keep their Ensemble small and concentrated, but then again, when individual motivation is lacking, extra bodies can outweigh natural losses in efficiency.

And we've also spoken to a number of Soloists who employ what we call the Shadow Ensemble. When Jen Klise of Target was recently trying to figure out how to dream up a cool new Web presence, she started by shooting an e-mail to a network of a dozen or so smart people she's met at companies far afield from Target: Microsoft, eBay, and Royal Bank of Canada. She was careful to ask them not how to solve her problem, but rather how they would consider it.

"My team at Target is small," says Klise. "We could never get these big results without these networks." Beyond her extended business network, Klise has a Shadow Ensemble in academics that includes designers and experts from Rhode Island School of Design and the MIT Media Lab.

SOLOIST FOR HIRE

For some companies, Bulldozers have run amok, Spreadsheets have everything tied up in knots, and Sheeple roam free. In such places, there may be no Soloists left to depend on to keep the corporation from settling into its deep-set ruts. Nature abhors a vacuum, which is why companies like Business Talent Group have begun to spring up. Based in Los Angeles, BTG has a roster of six hundred senior-executive types who can be air-dropped into short-staffed *Fortune* 500 companies in dire need of Soloist-style leadership. A quarter of the time, the transplanted project leader becomes a permanent addition to the company.

To judge by similar firms appearing around the country, this model is catching interest. Point B in Seattle has some four hundred troops ranged across seven cities. Each Soloist has ten to twenty years of executive experience heading up teams and leading projects – experience that is critical as these experts are sent out to run specific projects at industry-leading firms such as Microsoft, Starbucks, and the Gap.

Major companies have started turning to the outside because, while they often have capable managers, those roles don't always translate into Soloists. "We're like a general manager who is brought in to complete a project in three or six months, then it's on to the next company and the next project," one of Point B's roving project leaders told us. "There's a benefit to coming into a situation without any baggage or politics with the team to which you're assigned. At the same time, you have to rapidly assess how each of the members of the project team behave, separately and together. It's assessing that, then becoming the conductor of that orchestra to know how they all fit together."

SOLOIST TO SOLOIST

A true-blue People Hater may have trouble dealing with even a small, handpicked structure like an Ensemble, but if there's a Soloist bone in his body, he's still going to have the urge to merge – ideas, plans, or vision – with at least one fellow Soloist. It's just Soloist nature.

Earl Tupper was one such dyed-in-the-wool Soloist. Back in 1937, he bounced back from not making the grade as a tree surgeon and turned his attention to starting a plastic-molding business. He'd gotten his hands on as much cast-off polyethylene (a rubbery black by-product of the smelting process) as he wanted and started screwing around with it. Tupper heated it. Pressurized it. Mixed in different additives. Because it gave off no odor and was resistant to acid damage, he thought his "Poly-T" product might be good for storing food. By 1947, he had a patent and a new name: Tupperware. The only thing he didn't have was a way to get people to buy it.

Retailers couldn't move it because shoppers didn't know how it worked. Enter an ambitious Florida housewife who also happened to be a Soloist. Brownie Wise worked as an in-home distributor for another company, but by chance a friend gave her a piece of Tupperware. Impressed that the container didn't leak when dropped, Wise concocted the idea for home-based "Tupperware parties," hosted by homemakers for homemakers. Her innovation sparked a whole new way of selling products. Tupper was impressed and quickly made Wise vice president of his new company, and she became a sensation – and the first woman to grace the cover of *BusinessWeek* magazine.

Sometimes, that need to commingle ideas might happen quickly, while other times it might happen over the course of several years. The Soloists involved may not even come in direct contact with each other. The story of 3M's Post-it Notes is the stuff of innovative and creative legend. You may think you know the tale, but we're guessing you don't know the whole Soloist story.

In 1970, Spencer Silver was a researcher at the legendary 3M research labs. He'd been working hard to develop a superstrong adhesive. Unfortunately, what he ended up creating was weaker than the glues 3M already had in production. The new glue stuck to stuff but then could easily be lifted off. Another 3M scientist at the labs, Arthur Fry, had been trying to find a way to keep his paper marker in the hymnal he used in his church choir. He remembered Silver's lousy glue, got it out of the dark hole it had been dropped into, and – eureka! – it did the trick.

Here's the part you probably haven't heard. Fry didn't come up with his new application for Silver's invention for four years. It took two lone researchers, Soloists for sure, to take two discrete steps: first, create a new technology – weak glue – and then, much later, figure out an entirely new way to use it. That wasn't all. It took Ensembles and the might of 3M another six years before it started rolling out the Post-its in 1980 – a full decade after Silver's invention.

Although Soloists are not necessarily loners, the path can be a solitary one. Your efforts might be unsung, and people who think the workplace is about fostering friendships might label you antisocial. The trade-off is that you're learning how to find and keep the people around you critical to your success while those who would swipe your time, energy, and contributions are getting less and less of each. It won't take long to get your balance as a Soloist – to reach that place where you can do your work on your own terms and with fellow Soloists and Ensembles that make the job worthwhile.

The *Am I a Soloist?* Quiz

How do you know if you're a Soloist, or at least destined to become one? The easiest sniff test is how many times a day you mutter, shout, or even think to yourself, "I hate people!" But not all People Haters are necessarily Soloists.

This quiz will help determine the depth of your Soloist leanings. The higher your score, the more Soloist blood in your veins.

A. The portion of the day I prefer working by myself is . . .

    1. one hour.

    2. two hours.

    3. four hours.

    4. six hours.

    5. all day.

B. My favorite part of the day is . . .

    1. staff meetings.

    2. status meetings.

    3. dinner or cocktails with clients.

    4. lunch with colleagues.

    5. meeting with my boss.

C. I'm most comfortable working in a team with . . .

    1. ten or more people.

    2. seven to nine people.

    3. five to six people.

    4. two to four people.

    5. nobody.

D. An empty office makes me feel . . .

    1. creepy.

    2. lonely.

    3. unmotivated.

    4. at home.

    5. excited.

E. When I get to the office in the morning, I usually . . .

    1. bring in doughnuts and coffee for everyone.

    2. say hello to people and ask about their evening.

    3. nod to people I run into between the front door and my desk.

    4. grunt and head to my workspace.

    5. head to my workspace.

F. When I see an empty conference room, I think . . .

1. I hope I didn't miss the meeting.
2. I hope I set aside enough time for the meeting.
3. the meeting is about to start.
4. how can I get out of the meeting?
5. what a great place to write my report.

G. When I dream of the perfect office, I visualize . . .

1. a glass fishbowl in the center of the action.
2. the latest collaborative open-space environment.
3. small work-group offices.
4. a cubicle.
5. four walls and a door that locks.

H. The place I do my most creative work is . . .

1. at my desk.
2. in a meeting room.
3. in the break room.
4. at home.
5. outside.

I. I like a boss who . . .

1. checks up on me periodically.
2. asks what I'm working on in the morning.
3. gives me weekly assignments.
4. asks for monthly status reports.
5. rarely comes in.

J. I like a coworker who . . .

1. is friends with everyone.
2. regularly breaks up the day with office gossip.
3. freely converses during breaks and at lunch.
4. barely interacts with just a few people.
5. minds his own business.

YOUR SCORE

10–15 Forget it. You, my friend, are a teamworker, through and through.

16–25 Though more comfortable in a team setting, you occasionally like your alone time. Soloist larva.

26–35 Stretching your Soloist muscles. Yes, you like people a little too much.

36–45 Strong Soloist. You could be teaching others if you weren't spending so much time alone.

46–50 Cream of the Soloist crop. No one's getting in your way, and that's the way you like it.

6. Solocrafting

Hemingway, Bach, and Beethoven did it every day. Einstein did it during breaks at work at the patent office. Churchill did it better than perhaps any other politician. We've already met one of the modern masters of doing it – Craig Newmark. We'll be introducing you to more masters in the pages that follow.

What are we talking about?

Solocrafting. A natural by-product of hating people, it's all about setting aside the time to create. Rising early to write that Great American Novel. Staying up past the wee hours to work on your ninth symphony. Even slicing out a chunk of your afternoon to work in peace on a critical presentation. And then there's the natural side benefit of Solocrafting: the more you separate from the pack and pursue your solo tasks, the less time you spend with the people you hate.

It's the way a Soloist works, regardless of his profession. Solocrafting takes on many different forms. Most often you will be by yourself, though you can also Solocraft with an Ensemble or with one or two other Soloists. The key to Solocrafting is getting far enough away from interruptions and the forces behind them that you're able to work toward completing your goals.

Getting the real work done these days keeps getting shoved into the backseat by poorly planned projects, rampant meetings, and countless distractions. From consumer-products behemoths to tech giants, fire drills are the order of the day – mostly non-emergencies that divert attention because someone jumped into panic mode and got everyone else excited. Solocrafting is about the techniques and tricks to give the enterprising Soloist the ability to stay on top of his workload without toppling over.

But Solocrafting is far more than just smart time management. While we recognize that getting a handle on your day is important, Solocrafting goes beyond effectively using your time. There are many systems that purport to help you achieve this goal, from David Allen's Getting Things Done (widely known as GTD) to Tony Robbins's Rapid Planning Method to FranklinCovey's myriad organizers. None target the chief threat to your day: people. Solocrafting adds a vital element to your approach to productivity: it allows you to avoid, sidestep, or defuse the Ten Least Wanted and their ability to knock you off task.

Many professionals in major corporations Solocraft to stay current and exposed to new ideas and trends. "I still do freelance work on the side," says Kyle Johnston, Web and digital creative director at Garmin International. "I do websites for nonprofits and small companies." Johnston recently created a website for a local animal shelter. "It's a site with pretty good traffic, so I can experiment and take the things I learned there and apply them at Garmin." Johnston says these diverse jobs have given him a really good sense of what works. And like most corporate Soloists, he didn't ask permission to be creative. Johnston says that his Solocrafting and that of many others at Garmin fly under the radar at the *Fortune* 1000 company. "No one really knows that it's going on here, but the Web designers are all doing little side projects because they love designing."

Then there are people like Amol Sarva, an early employee at the hit Virgin Mobile, who has gone on to launch his own mobile firm in New York City, Peek. Though his daily responsibilities as CEO burn up a good twelve hours a day, Sarva has at least three other plates in the air. He takes time out during the week to advise friends on their startups. "Theoretically, there's some economic reward," he says, "but it's just fun to do." Sarva is also pushing through a multimillion-dollar condo project in Manhattan, where he says the rough-and-tumble world of construction has helped him in the more effete world of high tech. "I've gotten a lot better at slamming my fist," he says. "That's what people do in real estate to get things done. Just bang the table." Sarva says the construction world has taught him the value of doing whatever it takes. "I've gotten a lot of practical wisdom. There's been some real cross-pollination." And if that isn't enough to keep him busy, Sarva has started an Ensemble working on a wild new project that just might turn into another company that we'll talk about a little bit later.

Then there is the everyday Solocrafting of men like Dennis Boyle, the veteran studio head at IDEO, the leading design-strategy firm. By spearheading major innovations for industries as diverse as high tech and health care, Boyle has repeatedly shown the talent and spark that could easily make him a candidate for launching a startup, joining the core team of a promising new venture, or heading up a *Fortune* 500's research and development department. Yet Boyle fits nicely into our category of Stay-Puts, having remained fiercely loyal to the same firm for more than two decades and built an impressive career out of discovering fresh, imaginative ways to feed his interests and passions and build nests for other budding Soloists.

Consider just one of Boyle's creations: the IDEO Tech Box. Nearly every IDEO office has one: a gleaming cabinet and display overflowing with strange and wondrous materials, including a packet of supersaturated liquid that, with a twist, turns into a burning-hot solid; Nitinol, "memory metal" that reverts to its coiled shape when dunked in hot water; and Kevlar, the light material that can stop a bullet.

But while the Tech Box long ago became a corporate feature of IDEO offices, it began life as a cardboard box (or rather boxes) of junk under and around Boyle's cluttered desk. Ever since he was a boy in Ohio, Boyle had collected things that fascinated him, and by the time he moved west, his boxes were filled with exotic plastics, oddly molded parts, circuits, and fasteners. When he taught at Stanford, Boyle called it the "magic box" and encouraged his students to collect stuff that one day might prove inspirational.

When Boyle became an IDEO studio head, he had the epiphany that his messy hobby was a tremendous opportunity, a way to share new, unusual devices, parts, fabrics, and materials that might help with a design challenge or supercharge a brainstorm. Boyle decided the time had come to turn his crap into jewels. And just like that, with the help of an intern, his passions came out of his corner office and connected with others at IDEO, in a slick, inexpensive multi-drawered display.

At first, the company wasn't a big fan.

Even some of the Powers That Be at a forward-thinking place like IDEO made fun of Boyle's hobby. Some celebrated IDEO collectors were reluctant to join in his new communal exhibit. Sharing doesn't always come naturally. But the Stop Signs lost. The Tech Box became a runaway hit, one of the signature elements of an IDEO office. Variations on it quickly spread throughout the firm's international offices and became favorite stops on the IDEO tours that won over clients and earned the firm critical new work.

Seen another way, the Soloist's personal mess can be good for business. And sometimes, when business gets messy, only a Soloist can save the day.

A few years ago, Eric Brinker, the director of brand management and customer experience at JetBlue Airways, wanted to respond to customers' calls for healthier in-flight snacks. Brinker and his team decided to yank the "Munchie Mix," a blend of Doritos chips and other crunchy, salty bits. "It's the ultimate junk food," Brinker told *BusinessWeek* at the time.

Big mistake. JetBlue-flying junk-food aficionados went a little berserk. "This is the only reason I flew JetBlue!" was just one of the many "spirited letters" to flood the airline, according to Brinker. He figured that he'd better pull a U-turn, but was afraid his department might get gun-shy about trying innovations. The brave Soloist in him burst out, and he chose to make himself the target of a "Save the Munchie Mix" campaign on JetBlue's intranet. "Some pinhead in marketing decided to get rid of the Munchie Mix!" screamed the kickoff of the comeback effort. Embracing the humor of the situation, Brinker welcomed employees to crow the praises of Munchie Mix in poems and stories. Soon passengers had their salty snacks back, and Brinker's team had learned a valuable lesson: it's okay to make bold decisions. And if you're a Soloist, when things don't go according to plan, you'll have developed the confidence and skills to turn a crisis into an opportunity.

Solocrafting grows on you. The most extreme Soloists are often entrepreneurs, but you don't need to start a company to lead the interesting life of a Soloist. And if we do have the guts to launch that new business, it doesn't mean we're ready to stop going solo in the rest of our life. Because in the end, Solocrafting is as much about getting away from the people you hate as it is about getting stuff done. And you'll find an unexpected bonus. The more successful you become, the more you will need and crave solo time.

The art of Solocrafting is about how to be motivated, creative, and inspired in the face of the endless workplace distractions that can sideswipe your day. Peek behind the public image of nearly any successful person worth a damn, and you will find that the work that makes him or her famous often happens solo, behind closed doors, or with one or two other people. These men and women are religious about their Solocrafting. Whatever their passion, they're believers in the old adage "Write every day," admonishing novelists to put fingers to keyboard at least once every twenty-four hours.

But there's something deeper at work. By harnessing the power of hating people in a productive way, you're tapping into an extra dimension of time and space. A dimension free from the office, family, or community. A dimension where you can grab some deep thinking, meaningful creative exploration, or good old-fashioned goofing off. This is where Solocrafting happens, touching off those sparks that ignite great writing, inspire an awesome video game, or grow a market-bending business concept.

Perhaps the most interesting Soloists are those who operate within corporations, people working in less glamorous settings like Cargill – not the sort of corporation that normally shouts "innovation" or "Solocrafting." What started as a grain-storage joint almost a century and a half ago has swelled to become a global agricultural, food, and industrial-products behemoth.

In the late 1970s, Carol Pletcher, a bright young biochem PhD geek, joined Cargill in Minneapolis. Pletcher toiled fairly anonymously – just another human rat in Cargill's giant labs – and gradually worked her way up as a staff scientist and then manager. After roughly twenty years in the trenches, Pletcher became a VP, and, late in life, began to stretch her Solocrafting muscles.

Besides convincing Cargill management to bring in top-line innovative consultants, Pletcher created incentives for other Soloists to be rewarded for good ideas. She launched an innovation award program. The winners were invited to headquarters to get up on a stage, shake hands with the CEO, and give workshops to, yes, other Soloists.

Pletcher's next step was to identify and charge some six hundred talented individuals within Cargill with seeding other Soloists. It wasn't long before Carol Pletcher was crowned Cargill's chief innovation officer – quite a Soloist

BEGIN AT THE END

The blank page is the great fear of the novice Soloist. We've talked to dozens of people who say that this is the biggest obstacle in starting projects or spreading their Soloist wings. The empty Word document, PowerPoint slide, Excel spreadsheet — all are terrifying in their sheer blankness. The consultant Bryan Mekechuk has learned a simple but profound trick: he never starts from a blank sheet of paper. Mekechuk searches his hard drive and the Net for the closest thing to the document he has to write, the presentation he has to give, or the spreadsheet he has to develop. He says that it's not about pride of ownership. "If someone has done some other work, I want their ending point to be my starting point. It's worth spending the time finding that perfect starting point." He uses the ideas as a springboard for his own broader exploration.

honor, considering the company has one hundred thousand employees and more than $60 billion in annual revenues.

Since Pletcher began Solocrafting, Cargill has come up with some surprising new products, like a road salt designed to melt ice at lower temperatures that sticks to the road. But interestingly, Pletcher's tremendous track record didn't cause her to race off to launch her own company. Nor did she get fabulously rich. Despite earning a national reputation for championing innovation, Pletcher stayed on at Cargill for three decades, helping other Soloists find new solutions to the company's problems.

An ideal model for the Soloist is Wallace Stevens, one of the greatest American poets of the twentieth century.

Stevens didn't follow the traditional path of a man of letters, teaching at a university. Nor did he adopt the lifestyle of the tortured poet, toiling away in a dingy garret until dying of alcoholism or consumption. In a twist of People Hater irony, most of his life he worked as a corporate lawyer and an insurance executive – two of the most hated professions in history. Hardly a life that would seem to furnish the time or imagination to become one of the great modernist poets.

Stevens was an innovator tied down to some pretty straitlaced professions. Not to mention his loveless marriage. But he broke through, and not by yakking it up with his coworkers and getting heartburn over a heavy midday meal. Instead, nearly every lunch hour, he Solocrafted by fleeing the people he hated and shutting the door to his office to pen fantastic, wildly imaginative poetry. Then, after this brief flood of creativity, Stevens the lawyer and executive calmly returned to the business at hand.

A corporate lawyer to the end, he also won the Pulitzer a year before his death at seventy-six. It was that single hour at lunch, and undoubtedly many more Solocrafting hours snuck in after dinner and on the weekend, multiplied over his life, that gave him the time, concentration, and force necessary to write some of the greatest poems in our history.

Stevens's dull choice of a day job didn't stop him from finding the inspiration and time to Solocraft. Though poetry isn't generally the path to fame or success, over time he became celebrated and respected. That's not to say that your own hobby or pursuit needs to garner rave recognition or grow into some fabulous business opportunity. The important thing is that it gives your brain and energy a chance to recharge away from the work grid.

GIVE IT UP FOR GOOGLE

There are companies that get how encouraging Solocrafting on the job can turn into a victory for the Soloist and employer alike. Google is renowned for its "20 percent time," which gives engineers one day a week to pursue whatever projects spark their interest. Orkut Buyukkokten, who began working at Google in 2002, cooked up a social-networking program on his Soloist day. In 2004, Google launched the service publicly, christening it Orkut in honor of its developer. Today, the service is huge in Brazil and boasts millions of users around the world. No one's saying if Google pushed Orkut any big cash for his efforts, but for sure his 20 percent time has given him the fifteen minutes of fame Andy Warhol talked about: during a recent trek to Brazil, he was treated like a celebrity.

With all the glory Google has soaked up from celebrating just *one* Soloist's efforts, you're left to wonder why more "smart" companies aren't catching on faster.

Who knows? That home-brewed blog of yours might start to get several hundred daily hits. Or the video game you're programming at night could be just what Xbox needs. Or the murder-mystery novel set in an IT department you've been tapping away at could find a publisher. More than ever before in history, the odds are better that what used to be called "that thing Dad's working on in the garage" will become a business, a real source of extra income, a satisfying hobby – or the next big thing.

YOUR SOLOCRAFTING POWERPACK

Whatever your job or industry, one element is constant for the Soloist. You will need energy and passion to succeed at the highest level. What motivates us is personal. For some it might be excellence, while others crave recognition. Money never hurts.

But a job or a career is a battle waged over hours, weeks, and years. The veteran Soloist does his best to stay sharp even during that postlunch crash, when the urge to duck under the desk for a quick nap seems irresistible.

Remember Debbie Vargo, the P&G director? She's developed the discipline and strategy to stay balanced and committed as she enters her second quarter century at the company. Her personal program kicks off every business day at 4:30 a.m., with a run or power walk. On odd days, she lifts weights. But she doesn't stop with that morning jolt of exercise that has her ready for combat at her desk by 7:45 a.m. Vargo has a master's degree in food science and nutrition, and she puts her degree to work in picking the right fuel for her engine. "I eat in a way that keeps my glycemic index in check," she says, referring to her blood-sugar level. "That's enabled me to have the energy I need through the day."

Besides balanced meals of carbohydrates, protein, and some fat, Vargo eats a healthy midmorning and afternoon snack, making certain she's always got "five grams of protein for every one hundred calories." To those who think paying attention to how you eat throughout the workday doesn't sound businesslike, consider the typical alternative. The frantic executive who rises so late that all he's got time for is a quick shower, a Pop-Tart, and a Coke before slogging through traffic to the office. Then he shows restraint, only scarfing one bagel with cream cheese before his standard lunch: a hamburger with french fries . . . and another Coke.

In truth, the American worker profiled above is average, and considered normal by his employer.

But it's also true that it can be hard to resist the inexorable pull of the office meals and snacks. It takes tremendous courage and planning to eat sensibly when confronted with the weekly temptations: slabs of coworker birthday cake, pizza ordered on deadlines, shimmering fresh Danish adorning the conference table. And, of course, those fiendishly festive bowls of brightly colored candy scattered around the office.

The nutritional incompetence of many workers holds them back more than the absence of an advanced degree or talent. First, you skip breakfast and slam your body and brain into starvation mode. Pigging out at lunch, you spike your blood sugar, igniting the sort of irrational exuberance that bloats budgets and grasps at absurd marketing schemes. Equally troubling, you can count on this mania being followed by an early-afternoon coma.

More to our point, these junkie-style office highs and lows fuel People Hating. Institutional malnutrition messes with your mind and has an unpredictable effect on behavior. You may view a fellow staffer as a capable ally – except when under the influence of an afternoon Cheetos and snickerdoodles binge. Pour too much of that poison down an office gullet, and even a Gandhi might turn into a raging Bulldozer.

Then there's another problem. Dare to eat intelligently in the workplace, and you'll likely be mocked, humiliated, and ostracized. People who don't have your best interests at heart will announce, "How's that diet going, Bill?" while chomping down some potato chips.

Here's where the dedication of a Soloist serious about Solocrafting comes into play. Vargo of P&G does more than buffer her challenging mornings at the office with a dose of exercise-induced endorphins. Throughout the day, she literally makes certain her blood sugar stays within an optimum level. Vargo is one of countless modern office warriors who have taken charge of their health and fitness. She's completed the Corporate Athlete program at the Human Performance Institute in Orlando, Florida, headed by Jack Groppel. The program includes fitness, performance coaches, and nutrition. Vargo has gone on to train top women staffers at P&G's Miami Innovation Center, and she notes that while you can't get more than twenty-four hours in a day, "there are ways to maximize your energy."

Exercising regularly is not a prerequisite to Solocrafting. But more often than not, Soloists figure out how to balance their energy throughout the day. Little steps make a difference. Faced with regular, grueling five-hour meetings, Vargo doesn't take them sitting down. She stands for long stretches, not caring what others think. "Your heart rate goes up when you move from sitting to standing," she says. "It also breaks some of that tension."

SOLOCRAFTING IN MEETINGS

Teleconferences. Video calls. Face-to-face. Is there any kind of meeting that doesn't cause an involuntary shudder? Time squandered. Projects delayed. Calls unreturned. The wheels of productivity stuck in a corporate rut. As Elizabeth, a plain-talking public-relations manager at a major firm told us, "I hate the people who schedule meetings that are unnecessary. The meeting lovers. You don't need a meeting of sixty people to go over things, bit by bit, or state by state, or line item by line item. Many of these things could be done over a phone call or a visit to someone's cubicle."

Nicole, a marketing professional in the wine industry, put it even more starkly: "I hate the 'doing a meeting to set up a meeting.' Why don't we just talk now?" Even worse, she said, are the weak-kneed managers who go around the room in a show of wanting to hear everybody's opinion when they've already settled on the decision before they convened the meeting.

Fear of failure is a big reason why many companies drown their workers in get-togethers. In some companies, people are not rewarded for taking risks. "They're rewarded for not making mistakes," says Lisa Carmel, a veteran of British Petroleum and Procter & Gamble. "So it's easier to not make fast progress. They want to discuss it, discuss it, discuss it. If you meet, you set up another meeting to then investigate the learnings. Then you set another meeting."

Carmel says P&G was fairly stingy about meetings; not so with British Petroleum. "You could spend months just going to these meetings where nothing is ever getting accomplished. Going to a meeting, deciding what you need to investigate, and then putting off action." Carmel says one of the reasons she left BP for Procter was because she tired of the "do-nothing" endless meetings loops. She realized that for many people at BP it was an addiction. "There are these professional go-to-meeting people. Your whole day gets filled with meetings, and nothing gets accomplished."

Not surprisingly, we found plenty of bloggers eager to

rant on this subject, including Bill Gammell, host of the *überEye* marketing blog. The marketer claims to have found the seven signs of meeting addiction. Our favorite: "They start off the meeting by asking, 'Now, is this the strategic planning meeting or the budget meeting?'"

Sadly, meeting lovers rule many companies in America. Almost every successful manager, executive, and associate finds himself locked into daily meetings stacked up like jets over O'Hare. Yes, we all want "less meetings, more *doings*," as one project manager we talked to aptly put it. We know it's not feasible to ban the damned things like paper bags at the grocery store. But we do have ideas about how to Solo-craft during a meeting, serving two masters: your company and, more important, yourself.

The first step is to distinguish the meetings that require active participation – the meetings where you have to be on and can't miss a beat. You need approval for your new project. Increased funding. Or you have to deliver a presentation to upper management. There are also the meetings that you call. Obviously, you can't be caught slacking there.

But many meetings only require your passive involve-ment, and here lies your greatest opportunity for Solo-crafting. Today, a rising chunk of meetings take place by phone. So, what better time to get some extra work done than when no one else can even see you? Pete Johnson of Hewlett-Packard is directly responsible for several teams and hundreds of HP websites. He's an inveterate Soloist who makes time in his workday to play a game of Yahtzee with his daughter, but often must be in contact with the "mother ship" for twelve hours or more. Often half of that long day is consumed with phone conference meetings. A fifteen-year HP veteran, Johnson got clever about slicing off time for side tasks in a passive meeting. He can answer lots of two-second e-mails – "the ones short enough that you're not going to miss much."

While this technique is not recommended for face-to-face encounters, it can be useful for those participating in teleconferences. Many of our interviewees confessed to creatively taking advantage of the slow spots that crop up in meetings. Most seize these pockets of time to make progress on other work-related projects that they would otherwise fall behind on.

What about when you have to break off for longer stretches? Johnson's job includes keeping key HP websites online. Meetings or not, it's his job to respond to a site crash or some other glitch needing his immediate attention. If he can't pay attention during a meeting for five or ten minutes, he'll shoot a buddy (who's also attending) an IM: "What did I just miss?" Johnson says it's critical to cultivate buddies, both to IM for quick summaries and to cover for you. Think of these meetings as being in a foxhole with some of your closest chums. You watch each other's backs. Keep each other from getting fragged when things get rough.

You know: those deer-in-the-headlights moments. You just dashed off a quick e-mail and completely lost the thread of the meeting. Suddenly, over the phone, you get the Question: "Pete, what do *you* think?"

Johnson's no stranger to the Question. Throughout his career, he's had to think fast to have the right response. Here are a few of his techniques guaranteed to save your ass. Try not to use all three during the same meeting.

A . "I'm interested in what Joe thinks."

B. "Could you repeat the question?"

C. "I had to step away a minute to deal with an escalation. Can you catch me up?"

The key here is that Johnson's job requires him to Solocraft and juggle multiple tasks, especially during meetings. Depending on the situation, he may simply, as he puts it, "cop to the fact that I was doing something else." That's part of his job. Balance is key. If you routinely dump out of meetings, even on the phone, your passive meetings might suddenly start taking a turn toward the active. Good-bye, Solocrafting.

Take care to never confuse a passive meeting with an active meeting. People will hate *you* – and with good cause. If the meeting is in person, assume it's active. If you're expected to participate, it's active. If it's not the sort of meeting where people watch YouTube videos, check their Facebook page, and Twitter, it's active. One veteran executive we interviewed said he makes nearly all of his meetings short, and of the "all-in" variety. He says he's started many a meeting by looking around the table at the glazed eyes of attendees lost in the screens of their open laptops. "I'm the only one here without a laptop. Does this mean my time is the least valuable?" The clamshells close. It's all about focus. Having a laptop open is not multitasking. Says the executive: "That can turn a twenty-minute meeting into an hour."

Half an hour. That's all you need. That's what the majority of the executives and managers we talked to said is the maximum time needed for most meetings. Putting a stopwatch on the table is a start, but we have a more visible tool. Consider buying a "half hour" glass and setting it on the table. It's a rich metaphor: your life draining away one grain at a time. When someone starts blathering, make your point by just looking at the disappearing sand.

> *"Decision by democratic majority vote is a fine form of government, but it's a stinking way to create."*
>
> — LILLIAN HELLMAN

POOP ON MEETINGS

While everyone agrees there's a whole lot of meetin' going on, precious little time has been given to the time spent in meetings. One problem is that it varies from company to company, office to office, and job to job. Respondents to an online survey at www.management-issues.com said they typically spend more than a third of their workday in meetings and calculate that better than half of those didn't need to be called in the first place. Managers often report spending half or more of their day in face-to-face meetings or teleconferences. An HP manager we interviewed reported that he thinks nothing of being stuck in six to seven hours of meetings a day, while a veteran of Clorox said she clocks twenty-five hours a week. A vice president of product development we spoke with typically averages five or six scheduled meetings a day but says impromptu meetings often pump that to ten or more.

Bill Daniels, CEO of American Consulting & Training, which specializes in *Fortune* 500 management-group development, estimates that managers spend 40 to 60 percent of their time in meetings. More remarkable is that the people actually doing the bulk of the work – the employees – are stuck in meaningless meetings. "One of the real tragedies is that so many engineers are spending a huge amount of time in meetings," says Daniels. "Most companies are spending a third of their time and payroll in meetings with very little to show for it." Take just one style of meeting common at *Fortune* 500s: the quarterly work review. Daniels notes that at one corporation, the meeting consumed three days and absorbed twenty-five to forty attendees. Twelve divisions ran the same meeting that, over a year, cost the company roughly $1.5 million in wages. "One person after another doing PowerPoints – hundreds of them," says Daniels. "We've researched that and found that within a few hours after the meeting, almost nobody remembers what happened in the meeting."

Jen Klise of Target has developed a simple antimeeting rule that has afforded her many more hours a week to Solocraft. She declines invitations to attend recurrent meetings. "A lot of *Fortune* 100 companies have this calendar system where people can book you, and book you for the same meeting for every two weeks," says Klise. "I avoid anything that's reoccurring because it means not a ton of thought has been put into the meeting."

Saying no means that Klise runs against the tradition that a full calendar hikes your corporate status. She laughs at the notion that because her calendar is not crammed with endless meetings, "I don't look that important to others."

How do most businesspeople feel about all these meetings? Industrial and organizational psychologist Steven G. Rogelberg conducted a large study of meeting time on employee well-being. His odd conclusion: meetings aren't quite as awful as they seem. While a majority of those responding said that they were publicly negative about meetings,

Rogelberg reported that more people than expected viewed meetings as a positive part of the workday. This is like larger numbers of people than expected reporting that they don't totally hate driving around for half an hour looking for a downtown parking space.

And even that finding comes with a whopper of a catch. The people who get off on meetings are culled from the bottom of the business barrel.

Rogelberg reported that those whose personalities are "high in accomplishment striving," focused people who actually like to get things done, regard meetings as interruptions or, even worse, "barriers to getting real work done."

In other words, it's the losers in your office who *adore* meetings. They can look as though they're contributing without doing much of anything at all. And the more they meet, the busier they look. All while gaining "a greater sense of well-being," according to the study. Conversely, when the "get stuff done" people are forced to meet, their sense of well-being plummets. Most aggravating to the productive set are those frequent, short meetings that clot the day's flow with mindless, useless detail.

This finding is perfectly logical. After all, if people hate people one on one, multiplying the problem by a whole roomful of people is bound to be a disaster.

Fortunately, the mainstream business press has finally figured out that corporate meetings generally suck. In "The Seven Sins of Deadly Meetings," *Fast Company* quoted managers from a number of major corporations who believe that they waste untold millions of dollars on stupid get-togethers. Cisco Systems reported, "We have the most ineffective meetings of any company I've ever seen." Remarkably, a senior manager at Federal Express also fessed up: "We just seem to meet and meet and meet and we never seem to do anything."

In today's team-centric corporate mind lock, few ponder whether the problem might be meetings themselves. *Fast Company,* for instance, points to Intel as one of the few major companies that appears to conduct better meetings. The magazine concludes that the solution to bad meetings is good meetings. That's the nice solution.

We've got a more direct approach.

Kill meetings.

Companies waste millions of dollars and lose critical market opportunities because of ineffectual meetings. Wouldn't it be smarter to reexamine the whole failed routine? Focus on action as opposed to group navel contemplation?

A vice president at a *Fortune* 500 company has done the next best thing to mass execution. He's killed Friday meetings. Banned them entirely on the fifth day of the workweek, with this stated rationale: "So people can get their work done."

Funnily enough, the same veep (clearly a Soloist) spent the first few weeks of his meeting-killing campaign stopping staffers who just couldn't help themselves from having Friday meetings.

We admire his spirit and would like to take it even farther: add Wednesdays to the ban to give your project a midweek bump in productivity.

MOVING YOUR ENSEMBLE INTO YOUR OFFICE

One veteran executive we talked to who prefers to go by the name Lucy said that by the time she'd reached her sixth

Great Solocrafting in History

Case Study #1: Benjamin Franklin

Benjamin Franklin dropped out of school at age ten to work for his dad, making soap, a job that fortunately didn't last long. At twelve, Franklin was apprenticed to his brother, a printer. That's when the great thinker, inventor, diplomat, and ladies' man began to blossom into one of America's first great Soloists.

Franklin wasn't much for rules — a central Soloist trait. When his brother forbade the fifteen-year-old to write for his newspaper, Franklin began penning letters under the marvelous pseudonym Mrs. Silence Dogood. At twenty-one, he brought together a group of tradesmen and artisans, dubbed the Junto, with an eye toward bettering themselves and their community — a crude forerunner to Facebook. When the Junto found it difficult to afford the latest books, Franklin dreamed up the novel idea of the subscription library (a kind of low-tech Internet). The members pooled their funds to buy books, spawning the Library Company of Philadelphia, which became one of the world's greatest collections.

Franklin's inventions, writings, and diplomacy brought people and ideas together. He published a how-to best seller, *Poor Richard's Almanac*, filled with such great Soloist sayings as "Fish and visitors smell in three days," a fantastic Early American example of People Hating. Despite his public duties, he made sure to have plenty of solitude to solve whatever he thought needed solving — electricity, coming up with a better harmonica, and the Franklin stove.

Franklin's Solocrafting gave him the freedom to launch at least a dozen careers along with his countless inventions, including a tough-to-counterfeit banknote, which helped make him one of the only two non-presidents to grace a bill — the hundred, no less.

company, several of which had gone public, she'd fully cured herself of the "ask permission" passivity that chokes so many new projects in big companies. She had learned to just jump into what she calls her "beg forgiveness" mode.

When Lucy joined Genesys, the telecommunications firm, in 1999, she quickly discovered that the company had a big problem: it lacked any way to automate the installation of its computer telephony interface software. "I was told, Oh no, you can't do that," she said of the company's chief technical officer. "I was told it was impossible."

Soloists love to plow through Stop Signs. Lucy began pulling together her Ensemble. She grabbed a couple of engineers from the cubes and literally moved them into her office. She bought thousands of dollars' worth of computer servers and small cabinet-size telephone switches, transforming her office into a project center. Then she moved herself out of her own office, commandeering another space on the other side of the building. "Yeah," she chuckles, "I was a little hog."

Two cohorts expanded to half a dozen. There was barely room to walk around in the technology-stuffed office, and the hardware generated so much heat that Lucy's team had to install an air-conditioning unit. She did not have any official approval, but she kept her Ensemble marching forward. The Stop Signs in the company snickered. They figured she'd fail.

Several months later, Genesys was sold to Alcatel, and an executive from the firm paid a visit. He asked why the company couldn't do a quick install. Lucy promptly replied, "We're working on it right now."

Eight-member executive team in tow, she led everyone down to her Ensemble. Her nemesis stood outside the packed room and said it would never work. Then Lucy the Soloist showed the team the working prototype.

Just like that, she instantly became a hero.

NATURAL ENSEMBLE

At a downtown bar in a major city, we spoke to Emily and Scott, Soloists who work as traders for a major firm. We asked if they were part of an Ensemble.

EMILY: Me, him, and him [she pointed to another colleague and then to Scott]. We're [all] from Ohio.

SCOTT: We have a certain bond.

EMILY: Three of us out of eight. The three of us are the Ensemble.

SCOTT: We get all this bullshit pushed upon us, and then we [the Ensemble] talk about what really works.

EMILY: Just between us.

SCOTT: The realities. The realities of what works in the market.

EMILY: We sit next to each other. If I ever hear him talking stupid, I'll just say, "Uh, uh, sweetie, you're not saying the right thing." I just smack him and interject.

SCOTT: I'll listen to her because I know she knows what she's talking about.

EMILY: I'll smack him and tell him what's right. He's on a
   headset. And he's talking bullshit. I'll say, "That's not
   right."

SCOTT: I'm grateful for that.

EMILY: I just tell him what's correct. Don't lie. Don't BS. I'll
   hit him.

SCOTT: I'll be grateful. I'll be, like, "Great." Then I'll revise
   what I'm saying. I like her smacks.

YOUR "GET AWAY FROM PEOPLE" CARD

Solocrafting may make you rich, fit, and happy, or just help
you pay the bills. The key is that Solocrafting gives you a
socially acceptable reason to separate from the people who
sap your time and drive you crazy. Whether it's avoiding a
fifteen-minute nonurgent "emergency meeting" or skipping
another soul-draining lecture on approved requisitioning
techniques for new technology purchases, Solocrafting becomes your magic "Get Away from People" card.

This means different things to different people. Some
are forever concocting their ultimate exit strategy, whether
that means moving up in their current company or on to
another. Others desperately need to break away from
distractions to finish vital assignments that just aren't
getting done in the office. Or maybe you just need to
kick loose.

By beginning to create pockets of time and space to "go
Soloist" – time free from the drama and drag of your office
mates and the ceaseless agendas, meetings, and deadlines –
you'll find yourself making breakthroughs. Projects once
gathering dust suddenly gain traction with some thought-
ful introspection.

Solocrafting is personal. But these pursuits, and the valuable solo time they require, can be strengthened by teaming up with another Soloist. You can also form one or more Ensembles to help tackle various challenges. Perhaps what you need to get started is a writing partner for that screenplay or Web-based business, or a training buddy for that triathlon. Often that other person becomes another reason why the Solocrafting time is sacrosanct. And sometimes you just need a partner to kick you in the ass.

DIVISION X

Try something more ambitious with an office buddy. Once or twice a week, go out for lunch together and brainstorm on Division X. It's a great way to get your Ensemble together.

You haven't heard of Division X? Every company has at least one. It's a new, top-secret department with some very cool ideas. Once you start gathering momentum, you might invite a third trusted person and build up some critical mass. No, Division X doesn't exist quite yet, but fanciful as it may sound, what we're describing is actually a proven method for starting new initiatives or projects within big companies. Why the off-site initial Solocrafting? Why stay off the radar in the early going? You've got to generate enough momentum and mass to survive the inevitable ruckus raised by the people most likely to get in your way.

Soloists at every level of their companies are exploring their Division X. Amol Sarva, the CEO of mobile startup Peek, works long days, yet he pursues what he calls "hobbies" that refresh him during the week. The latest is an exploration of a new business to tackle electronics recycling. He's created his own Division X, an Ensemble made up of the head of the New York office of the design firm IDEO, an executive at Target, and a man who has his own company. "We're bouncing ideas off each other. It's fun to work on," Sarva says, adding that while he's kept his Division X totally separate from Peek, it could ultimately have benefits for the company.

> *"You are remembered for the rules you break."*
> — GENERAL DOUGLAS MACARTHUR

UNTANGLING THE HAIRBALL

Gordon MacKenzie was an archetypal Soloist who decided it was more fun to Solocraft from within. The late MacKenzie is beloved for his cult business classic, *Orbiting the Giant Hairball,* but his career is almost more instructive than his coolly rebellious book. MacKenzie was once a bohemian artist and cartoonist who eventually decided that a paycheck and a pension could be useful, and took a job with Hallmark. His title was "creative paradox," his assignment "to create for the company." The trouble, he wrote, was that "there was not a day when I was not subject to the inexorable pull of Corporate Gravity tug, tug, tugging me toward . . . the tangle of the Hairball, where the ghosts of past successes outvote original thinking."

MacKenzie's book describes how he learned to expertly orbit the Corporate Hairball. As with so many great books, no publisher wanted it at first, but then it became a business classic. It's missing just one thing.

Gordon MacKenzie was a very diplomatic man who, perhaps because he worked at a greeting-card company, could not say what we can: people hate people.

Creative people probably hate more than most. Why? They've got more invested. They know Stop Signs and Spreadsheets hold them back. And they're certain the world needs their ideas and new products.

MacKenzie wrote humorously and eloquently on the Corporate Hairball and the rules and unspoken unwieldy practices and groupthink that gum up large organizations. He tiptoed around the people who are the hairs in the Hairball. But he was a brilliant Soloist within Hallmark: "I emerged from the Company Cocoon. Slipped the bonds of the Hairball of Corporate Normalcy. Ascended into Orbit." MacKenzie became a champion of autonomy. He was the man you'd call if your great idea became stuck in the Hairball. Say that Bulldozer in management blew out your project. Or that Switchblade Stop-Signed you on the drawing board, or a picky Spreadsheet in accounting said she wouldn't foot the bill for the antique milk cans you want for your hot new Ensemble. MacKenzie worked exactly thirty years at Hallmark, a model Soloist who discovered a major key to Solocrafting within an organization.

Gordon MacKenzie and Carol Pletcher are unlikely giants in the pantheon of corporate Soloists. But Solocrafting comes in many forms. Maybe you've figured out a way to offer up funny videos to the world and sell the website to Google for a billion dollars. Fantastic – but it's also pretty cool if you learn ceramics at a night class and find that somehow it makes you more creative and successful as a graphic designer. Or discover that training for a triathlon's three events helps you handle the multitasking stress of your job.

Solocrafting turns a Soloist's natural inclination to hate people in groups into individual sprints that deliver results. What's more, you'll find other Soloists coming out of the woodwork. When someone ends up not having a meeting because you're unavailable, he may just find the extra time gives him the chance for a little Solocrafting of his own.

SOLOCRAFT ENABLERS

Whether you're considering starting up Division X or are just signing up for that photography class, there's always that first step. Maybe you've got to write a check for a class or stand up in front of the group and show your work.

Sounds pretty straightforward, but there's one little problem. We've been told since elementary school what we can't do. So, of course, we're doomed to fail before we even get started. Couple that with our usual nearsightedness about making money, earning popularity, or otherwise creating distinction or success, and it's a wonder anybody ever gets around to doing anything.

Looking at being a Soloist through a child's eyes is a great idea. Why do kids get so excited about so many activities, from playing sports to performing in a play to finger painting? Because they are doing more than thinking about the results. Because they don't suffer the dark reality of end-term adult think that destroys what little remains of childhood. And they're not afraid to admit that they hate people.

"I hate you!" Sound familiar?

Kids don't get bored or stuck for long. They skip on to something else until they find fresh inspiration and return with newfound enthusiasm. They're acting in the play, as opposed to thinking about whether they'll get a TV role one day and make a living as an actor. Which is how we grown-ups tend to stop things before we even get started.

Great Solocrafting in History

Case Study #2: Tom Sawyer

Our Soloist literary example is the beloved character from several of Mark Twain's books, who personified the Soloist by convincing others how much fun it would be to complete the mundane task he'd been assigned: whitewashing the fence in front of his house. And what of Tom Sawyer's attitude toward people? Mark Twain had this to say: "He was not the Model Boy of the village. He knew the model boy very well though — and loathed him."

SOLOCRAFT SYNERGY

Once you Solocraft, you often find that, along with getting away from the people you hate, there's a synergy and a collective force in doing all these separate solo pursuits.

Consider Marc Hershon's late father, Norm. He loved going to Bay Meadows, the old race track south of San Francisco. It wasn't so much to place bets, but just to hang around the ponies, the jockeys, the thrilling world of thoroughbred racing. His day job was Northern California ad manager for *TV Guide* magazine. Somewhere in the back of his mind, he was wondering how he could spend less time in the stuffy office and limiting world of ad sales and more time in the open air of the sport of kings. His attention was drawn to the closed-circuit TVs placed throughout the stands and betting windows, where people could watch the horses even when away from their seats.

Norm noticed that when the two-minute races weren't running, the screens were blank. He went to Bay Meadows management with an idea. He'd sell ads to put on the screens. Great, said the track. Within weeks of hatching his scheme, Norm dropped the same idea in the lap of Golden Gate Fields, the other track across the bay, and it, too, eagerly climbed aboard. Soon his hobby was generating some serious extra income.

A few years later, Norm hit the Soloist's version of the exacta. After two decades in the same position at *TV Guide,* he catapulted himself out of the magazine biz and turned his hobby into his dream job, head of public relations for Golden Gate Fields.

This is Ultimate Solocrafting: a hobby or pursuit that literally propels you to a novel career or more satisfying life. It often gives you relief from the people and the things you hate (a dull office environment, irritating coworkers, tiresome relations). Solocrafting is its own reward, but stick with it, and other benefits often flow naturally. Happiness. Money. New job opportunities.

Whether you work for a small company or a giant corporation, Solocrafting lies within your grasp. Dave Cummings's unlikely career began at Cerner, the multibillion-dollar health-care IT company headquartered in his hometown of Kansas City. His story is evidence that anyone, anywhere, can become a serious Soloist.

The young programmer seemed to have found the mother ship when he got a job at the premier corporation. Cummings did fine at Cerner but began to wonder if he was made to be a corporate cog. "When one of these edicts would come down from upper management, I'd find myself laughing," he recalls. "They'd just be so arbitrary. I couldn't believe how many people would jump and reorder their whole life because the company said so."

Cummings jumped in a whole different direction. He took little steps as a Soloist that added up to giant leaps. Cummings thinks one reason people in many big companies do things they hate themselves for – moving to cities they detest, carrying out orders that go against their ethics, staying in dull jobs – is basic economics. He thinks a good part of Solocrafting boils down to money.

By his early twenties, though earning only a reasonable salary, Cummings had put away a year or two in living expenses. Feeling less dependent on Cerner gave him the confidence to leave his job and take a spin at Solocrafting. Cummings taught himself to become a commodities trader at the Kansas City Board of Trade. His modest goal: to make $100,000 a year. Once he accomplished that, he realized that a computer program could help him execute more than twenty-five trades a day. Working out of his bedroom, he designed a program that could enable him to make thousands of trades a day. His first company, Tradebot, was born, but it was just the beginning. In the summer of 2005, Cummings watched NASDAQ gobble up two upstart, competitive electronic exchanges. He believed monopolization was bad for free trade. So he launched his second Solocrafting beast, a new electronic exchange provocatively called BATS Trading Inc.

But Cummings had no real clients. New York's brokerages and hedge funds weren't exactly banging on his Kansas City door.

So Cummings banged on theirs.

He began firing off little manifestos, weekly e-mails dispatched to potential users of his burgeoning exchange.

Cummings was no professional writer, but he admired a good sermon and was fascinated with storytelling. A fan of Walt Disney, another man with Kansas City roots, Cummings understood that every good story needs a hero – and a villain. "The little guy comes out on top," he says. "That's Storytelling 101."

And so Dave Cummings, only a few years removed from being destined to a lifetime of corporate cogging, did the programming equivalent of an interrupt.

He broke the code.

Cummings's e-mail dispatches announced BATS's plans and, more important, tweaked Goliath. Cummings made fun of NASDAQ's CEO, Robert Greifeld. Called him "Bob the Bully." Trashed NASDAQ as a "monster" for trying to squelch competition in order to jack up prices. Only about thirty men on Wall Street received his first few epistles. "But people wanted to hear what I was saying," recalls Cummings. "Suddenly, twenty more asked to be added to the list." Soon a thousand top executives and traders on Wall Street had requested to be added to his weekly mailing. Cummings was tackling real issues head-on. "There was overconsolidation in the industry and we had to fix that," he says. "We were creating a new market center."

But that's just the half of it.

Cummings's folksy straight shooting appealed to Wall Street, a skyscraping realm given to labyrinths of double-talk. *Forbes* and the *Economist* chronicled his feisty efforts. He turned his weekly e-mails into a mission and a game. It all felt like a hobby. A fan of both Bill O'Reilly and Jon Stewart, Cummings had a formula: "Always have one or two good lines. Something a little edgy. Something people will want to repeat."

Cummings's e-mail blasts were soon read by tens of thousands in the industry, earning him paying customers and big investors. Lehman Brothers, Morgan Stanley, and Merrill Lynch bought into his exchange. All because he had the guts to say in a good-natured way that he hated Bob the Bully and his monopolistic exchange.

It helped that Cummings was funny. His humor and the appeal of his business got the market's attention. "The brokerages were feeling the same pricing pressures," he says. "I chose to speak my mind. To say what I thought. And let the chips fall where they may."

Not a bad philosophy for a Soloist ready to crack the mold.

QUICK 10

Sure, Solocrafting sounds great. But as with most professionals, your day is often fractured by interruptions. What you need is a bulletproof chunk of your workday. You need a Quick 10. Shave off ten minutes – say, from 11:00 a.m. to 11:10 a.m. – with no interruptions allowed. Period. No phone calls. No visitors. No e-mails. Here's a little secret. Believe it or not, apart from a sudden late-night birth or a three-alarm fire, most "emergencies" can wait ten minutes.

Establish this pattern over the course of a week. At 11:00 a.m. every day, announce you're taking a Quick 10. If you need an official reason, say it's to catch up on work, fine-tune a report, return e-mails. Whatever. But action is the strongest course. Ultimately, the magic of your Quick 10 is that it's your business.

When people interrupt, tell them how it's going to be: "I'm in the middle of my Quick 10. I'll be right with you." What's next? Test the waters. See how many more precious minutes you can grab for yourself before the interruptions overwhelm your dam. Maybe in a couple of weeks, your Quick 10 becomes a Quick 20. If you're really skilled, in a month, you've gained a quick half hour.

At this point, you're likely pushing your luck. Most folks don't understand the value of a Quick 10 and are constantly interrupting and being interrupted. The Quick 10 methodology requires time to take root. Once your immediate coworkers realize there are ten minutes when you're not interrupting them, the clever ones will see the light and want their own Quick 10.

After you succeed at carving out your Quick Half Hour, the smartest move is often to aim for a second session in the afternoon. Pick a time in the back half of your day, say, 3:00 p.m., to grab another Quick 10, and gradually build up.

Why does this work? First, it announces that what you do is important enough that for some period during the day, you cannot be interrupted. It takes guts, discipline, chutzpah – stones, if you will – to mark off this time territory.

Some will resent your new freedom and come at you from a variety of angles. Minute Man will want those minutes for himself. Bulldozer will try to bully you out of taking the time. Flimflam will try to fool you into doing a specific task that will benefit him during that time. Relax. Yes, you may need to devise special strategies for one or two of the Ten Least Wanted. But most of the people wanting to horn in on your Quick 10 will soon tire of the game and move on to more susceptible victims.

Hold tight. But if someone barges into your office and wants to talk during your time, don't rudely blow him off. Let him know that you'll connect with him as soon as you can – following your Quick 10.

Bosses, of course, are another category. They have an uncanny knack for "needing you" at the most inopportune times, and require the most training and careful handling. But the smart bosses will gradually recognize that your Quick 10, however long it becomes, is a benefit to everybody.

Remember, imitation is the sincerest form of flattery. Feel free to let your boss take credit for inventing the Quick 10 productivity concept – which in his case will quickly stretch into an hour.

So what do you do with your Quick 10? Early on, just bask in the freedom. Own it. Make it yours. Maybe you'll drink some coffee from a real mug. Read the *New York Times* or Yahoo! Sports, or catch a YouTube video. Perhaps you'll work on your fantasy-football team or write a page of that movie script. Pop a few push-ups. And there's nothing wrong with getting some solid work done.

Warning Signs You Need a Quick 10

▶ If it's 11:00 a.m. and you realize you'd have made more progress on the report due at noon if you'd just stayed on the subway and been to Brooklyn twice, you need a Quick 10.

▶ If you've just returned from vacation and your e-mail inbox is so jammed that you turn the automated vacation notice back on, you need a Quick 10.

▶ If you're getting phone messages from the people who called about the phone messages you got about the phone messages you didn't return last week, you need a Quick 10.

► If your boss keeps setting arbitrary deadlines for projects that you both know don't have to be done until the end of the month, you need a Quick 10.

► If just one more person sticks his face in your cube before lunch, and you want to rip it off with a staple remover, you need a Quick 10.

If your boss or company finds concentrated solo work a radical concept, you might consider countering with this fact: a Harvard Business School study has offered compelling evidence of the effectiveness of a Quick 10. While exploring the work-time cycles of a gaggle of software engineers, professor Leslie Perlow tested stretches of "quiet time" against "interaction time." Fifty-nine percent of the engineers reported that their productivity was above average – rating a 4 or 5 on a 5-point scale – versus when they had to work with others. During the interactive times, productivity sagged to a rating of 2 or 3 out of 5. Clearly, hacking off a hunk of quiet time in the form of a Quick 10 has productivity benefits.

We've talked to a number of professionals and executives who have made a variation on the Quick 10 central to their process. They break down their entire workday into discrete Quick 10s. "I have a fifteen-minute rule," says a veteran executive. "In that fifteen minutes, I get an hour of productivity." He applies his fifteen-minute rule to all sorts of tasks: concentrated Solocrafting, meeting briefly with an Ensemble member on a project, talking over company finances with the CFO. His idea is simple and powerful. Work on projects in concentrated bursts of roughly fifteen minutes, and then jump to something different.

The executive has promoted his Quick 15 at many of the companies where he's worked, and he says he can judge someone's productivity by what he can accomplish in fifteen minutes. "Some people I've worked with would spend a lot of hours at the office and not accomplish much. I attribute that to not following the fifteen-minute rule." He's no absolutist. Sometimes his Quick 15 only takes 5, and every once in a while, he may devote twenty to twenty-five minutes to a single task. But he claims to have timed it out to the point where fifteen minutes is pretty darn good. "That's how long it takes to make a point and move the ball down the field," he says. Staying with it longer usually isn't worth it. "Make a decision. Call it a day. Or move on to something different."

A point of clarification: some of you may already be hip to ducking out of the office for twenty or thirty minutes. We're all in favor of that maneuver, but it's no replacement for an honest-to-goodness Quick 10. Why? By demanding time for yourself while you're in the office during the normal chaotic jumble of business, you're establishing your beachhead. Once you assert that visible in-your-face dignity, it's difficult for anyone to take it away from you. That increased authority will make it that much easier to Solocraft outside the office.

As you begin to grow more comfortable in your Quick 10, and the office starts to respect your solo time, your confidence will grow, and you'll begin to actively plan for whatever it is you want to accomplish in your time. You'll become more efficient. More attuned to the interruptions that pull at your concentration all day – the ones that can be deflected for minutes, hours, or days. And more attuned to the precious few that demand immediate attention. This is a visible skill in the organization. You will rise in stature. Day by day, you are becoming that quarterback who remains unruffled, even when a posse of 350-pound linemen is bearing down on you.

Solocrafting is a skill. Whether you're an experienced Soloist or just starting down the path, you can begin applying the principles. The first step is simply breaking off from the pack. Making time for a Quick 10. Spending less time in bullshit meetings. Getting together with like-minded Soloists on your lunch hour. Launching an Ensemble. If you're more the entrepreneurial sort, like Dave Cummings, you can begin mapping out your route in the next few years. Or if you're happy where you are, like Carol Pletcher, you can start customizing your corporate nest.

The better you Solocraft, the less time and energy you waste on the people you hate. You've begun to systematically reduce the number of people and situations that drag you down. You're seizing control of your productivity rather than having to wait for randomly clear moments to pop up.

It's a journey that begins one morning at the office. You finally say no — to distractions, inane meetings, and irritating interruptions. Begin to say yes to a new way of working, both alone and with others.

Solocrafting.

THREE

OFFICE LIFE

7. Running Interference

"The average American worker has fifty interruptions a day, of which seventy percent have nothing to do with work."

— W. EDWARDS DEMING

Whether you're a CEO or a project manager, you likely face a nonstop onslaught of interruptions. Unrelenting attempts to reach you. Wave upon wave of e-mails, text messages, phone and cell calls. Every shade of interruption. Day and night. Seven days a week. Three hundred sixty-five days a year.

Endless.

One recent study demonstrated that workers spent 50 percent more time managing e-mail in 2006 than they did in 2003 – more than a quarter of their day. Today, experts estimate that the average corporate user fritters away 40 percent of his day dealing with e-mail.

Countless studies have shown how unchecked communications cripple productivity. The wasted hours. The loss of concentrated work. People hate it, but most of us haven't figured out how to break free.

Researchers have done a lot of thinking about interruptions. To prove it, they came up with this absurdly long jargon-filled term to describe the phenomenon: an "externally generated, randomly occurring, discrete event that breaks continuity of cognitive focus on a primary task."

You know, people getting in your face when you least need or expect them. CubeSmart, a company devoted to making your cubicle a more work-happy, productive environment, maintains that the average office worker is interrupted seventy-three times every day. The average manager has to put up with unexpected intrusions every eight minutes.

While it's nice to take an unscheduled break, uninvited disruption in your workday can be maddening. Especially when most people are fielding six or seven of these knuckleballs an hour. Five minutes is how long most interruptions last. Try that math on for size: say you get seventy five-minute interruptions a day. That's nearly six hours. Two-thirds of your eight-hour workday is gone. Eaten up by random folks horning in on you and your precious time.

A few interruptions are welcome. They can even be crucial. But they're in the minority. Trivial nonsense forms the bulk of disruptions. Only about 20 percent of the interruptions are typically considered crucial or important. So there you are, frittering away more than half your day on things you're better off ignoring.

But these figures only calculate the immediate cost of the interruptions. The worst part is the recovery time. Getting back up to speed on . . . what was it you were working on just before your phone rang? Damn. Should have jotted it down. Half the time, getting revved back up to where you were takes up to five minutes. Nearly 40 percent of the time it can be fifteen minutes before you're back up to speed. With the more noxious interruptions, regaining your focus can demand up to half an hour.

> *"The effectiveness of work increases according to geometric progression if there are no interruptions."*
> — ANDRÉ MAUROIS (1885–1967)

When your universe is the cube farm, this gets even more mucked up. On top of your seventy-three daily interruptions, you're also tangling with your neighbors' seventy-three daily interruptions. You may not be taking the phone call, answering the e-mail, or dealing with the drop-in visit by the boss, but you are in range. You can't help but momentarily check out of what you're doing to make sure whatever is happening doesn't somehow demand your attention. Every second off your task requires a recovery phase, making it nearly impossible to establish a productive work flow.

How do all these interruptions slice up your day? Researchers from the Department of Informatics at UC Irvine and the Institute of Psychology at Berlin's Humboldt University recently conducted a study to find out.

They began their investigation with the assumption that interruptions related to the task at hand would be less disruptive than those that yank you completely out of your zone. But contrary to expectations, the study showed that a disruption is a disruption. They all cost you time and lost concentration.

Another surprise: interrupted work tends to be performed *faster,* not slower, as was first believed. People in environments jam-packed with interruptions accelerate to compensate for the time they know will be lost to interruptions. Speeding up to cope with interruptions heaps on added work, stress, and frustration, not to mention the extra effort and pressure. Even worse, the negative effects begin kicking in after just *twenty minutes* of interrupted performance.

"Work fragmentation" is what the professors called it. In a follow-up study, UC Irvine researchers observed the breakneck pace of IT workers at a Southern California company. Apparently, the interruptive work style is contagious. Even when people weren't interrupted by others, they would abruptly switch tasks on their own. People worked only about eleven minutes before they were either interrupted or voluntarily changed tasks. They might interrupt themselves to do other projects or, incredibly, just to organize their e-mail. Not read or answer it: *organize* it. And sometimes they'd just lose their place. "You forget what you are working on, so you kind of do something else for a while, and then you remember what you're working on," said one of the study's respondents.

Interestingly, the right attitude and demeanor can help create a Soloist sanctuary. The study showed that frequent interrupters thought nothing of regularly bothering their cubemates if they seemed available. But when they seemed busy, they'd leave them alone or ask if it was okay to interrupt. Clearly, if you don't want to be interrupted, looking and sounding busy is your best defense.

But while that strategy may work for fending off your cubies, electronic intrusions are another matter. The torrent of e-mail messages and calls force our fingers into a modern form of electronic slavery – twitching our way into busywork, foolish confrontations, and downright hostility. There are days when the volume of e-mail alone is enough to make us shriek. Who can really answer – or deal with – two hundred messages in a day? Three hundred? Five hundred?

Everybody gets hammered by e-mail. Yet we're incredibly stupid about it. We can't help ourselves. We're curious by nature. Even as we find ourselves dragged into this digital morass, we can't help hoping that we'll stumble upon a gem. We begin each day naively hoping that among the hundreds of mundane, irritating, and misspelled pieces of e-trash – we're not even talking about spam – will be the Message. A promising new contract, good news from a client, confirmation of payment.

The challenge is the enormous volume, and it's not likely to get much better.

The people who make the software are happy to keep drowning us in e-mail. The only time they grant us an e-mail holiday is when we're on vacation. You know, the e-mail vacation notice. The shortsighted idea that the only time you don't want e-mail is when you're out of the office. How about a notice for when you're in the office but too busy working to answer the e-mail that keeps pouring in? The software already exists. Simply customize it to fit your work style. It's a question of behavior. Stand up and order your work life in a manner that makes sense and gives you the space, time, and freedom to succeed.

A number of executives told us that they've effectively given e-mail some of the old-fashioned treatment of regular mail. They decide in advance on fixed "delivery times."

> ## You Can Keep Your Hat On
> ———
> We believe in a direct, personal approach to reducing disruptions, one that takes a Do Not Disturb sign with you throughout the office. Consider this story of a former editor at the *San Jose Mercury News* who found herself being interrupted all day long and unable to get her work done. Journalist Don Fry came up with the solution: he bought her a red baseball cap. The staff was then told that the editor was totally available to them . . . except when she wore the red hat. Within six months, the staff had been trained, and the editor found she only needed about twenty blissfully uninterrupted red-hat minutes a day to get her stuff out of the way.

They read e-mails at 8:00 a.m., noon, and 5:00 p.m. – and never in the evening. We think this is an excellent strategy. We just want to take it one step farther. Why not tell people up front how much time you have to trade keystrokes with them today?

Our solution is to hang a new virtual shingle over your electronic office door. The "Yeah, I Got Your E-Mail But I'm Really Really Really Busy Right Now" notice. Make this message as straightforward or lighthearted as you like. Simply broaden your use of today's existing vacation-notice software and create your own custom message.

Daily E-Mail Vacations

▶ If you're an obsessive-compulsive and can't help but respond to e-mail within ten minutes, set it to ***Right Back at Ya***.

▶ If you want to take some time but don't want to feel guilty about it, give yourself an hour or so with ***Hold That Thought***.

▶ If you're so ambitious that you'll actually be able to return e-mail before lunch, use ***I'll Get Back to You Before I Stuff My Face***.

▶ If the best you can possibly hope for is to return e-mails before you leave for the day, try ***I Said I'd Get Back to You!***

▶ If none of the above give you enough time to get your work done, consider the classic ***E-mail Out of Order***.

It's an attitude. And a lot smarter than the recent practice we've noticed of simply leaving your vacation notice on long after you've returned. Create your own phrases to suit the style of your business and the demands of the day. Start exhibiting this discipline at the office. Your degree of e-mail responsiveness is completely flexible. It depends on what you need to get done on any given day and how much interrupting you can stand.

If pushing back with custom vacation notices is a bit too extreme, chat up a pal in IT. Ask him to do a little job on the signature function of your e-mail app: the code that lets you hang your name and business info at the bottom of every outgoing e-mail. It's totally customizable.

Create one that says "I just got your e-mail. I'll get back to you tomorrow. Thanks!" Or something similar, in your own tone. You can create as many custom replies as you want, then use the function keys to select them: F1 for "I'm swamped – try to get back to you by the end of the week," F2 for "I'm traveling – get back to you by the end of the week."

The catastrophe of e-mail glut has already brought us the oxymoron of e-mail productivity tools. As we write this, Seriosity of Palo Alto is beta-testing Attent, a tool that applies virtual economics to e-mail messages. Attent ranks the value of messages with virtual currencies. The aim is to train workers in how to effectively prioritize their electronic missives.

Whether Attent or something similar catches on, there's no doubt that we're going to have to get a whole lot more discerning about who and what to ignore during the business day.

Too bad e-mail is just one of the intrusions that splinter your day.

> *"Noise is the most impertinent of all forms of interruption. It is not only an interruption, but is also a disruption of thought."*
>
> — ARTHUR SCHOPENHAUER (1788–1860)

CELL PHONES

Early in the twentieth century, the telephone was a relative novelty, like telegrams and spats and button shoes. There was nothing private about making a call at the office. You'd connect to the company switchboard, where a woman (it was always a woman) would literally plug your line into an outgoing line and connect you to another operator, who would complete the connection. This was time-consuming. Inconvenient. And there was only one ringtone.

By the late 1980s, cell phones made their American debut. They were ridiculously expensive, clunky, and unreliable. That all changed within a decade, along with personal calls at the office.

For the first time, nobody could listen in. No office operator. No nosy coworker picking up an extension. Your mobility meant you could go where no one could eavesdrop. It was a little bit like an adult walkie-talkie. We all became secret agents. We were James Bond, Mata Hari, Dick Tracy. We fell in love with the cell phone. And we got an endless number of ringtones.

Cells have evolved and taken on personality. They play music and games. Snap photos. Show videos. Send and receive text messages. Everyone's got one: the latest figures put wireless service at nearly 90 percent of the U.S. population. A funny thing has happened getting here: making that personal call at the office is no longer on the company's dime. Old prohibitions have become unenforceable. Now keeping cell phones silent within company walls has become impossible. They're everywhere. The key is to define your relationship with your cell phone. Let's begin by finding ourselves along the spectrum of cell phoners. Do you use it as an ear extension, or do you have trouble remembering to keep it charged?

OLD FARTS

Old Farts tend to be fifty-plus, but the defining characteristic is that they rarely turn their cell on. Yes, you may take it to work. Might even remember your number. But you almost never receive calls in real time, and are surprised when you *do* switch it on and discover – hey! – you have v-mail . . . which you can't remember how to retrieve. Old Farts find the cell habits of others irritating. They get pissed when colleagues' phones go off during a meeting. Furious when, while talking to a colleague, he has the gall to take a call midconversation. Old Farts don't like people who like cell phones. Secretly, they keep hoping the damn things are just a passing fad. Like the Hula-hoop. This puts them on the wrong side of the bell curve and dooms them to pointless hostility (what we call dumb hate). If you suffer from Old Fart tendencies, snap out of it . . . at least at work.

ADOPTERS

Characterized by a willingness to pick up or adopt new technology and customs, Adopters typically range from their midthirties to midforties. Younger and older eager Adopters also fit this archetype. Adopters aren't cool, but they don't know it. They get dozens of calls a day, but they're still trying a little too hard. Texting hurts Adopters' thumbs, and they don't get the abbreviations. They feel guilty talking on their cell at their desk, but they still leave it on. Adopters get the cell-phone "intimacy factor." They're comfortable talking to clients and associates via cell in a variety of settings (driving, walking down the street, at a restaurant, working out). This intimacy factor allows business friendships to spring up with people they may never meet face-to-face. What's the difference between a hardline phone and a cell? Adopters are able to invite these business friends along with them into nearly every aspect of their lives. The borders that used to narrow our hardline conversations — you were sitting at your desk, she was sitting at her desk — have evaporated. Adopters take their newfound friendships even into the restroom, but they still haven't quite gotten up the courage to talk on their cell while taking a dump.

24/7s

They don't turn it off. Ever. Monday through Sunday, noon and night. Get it? The 24/7s tend to be subthirty, though increasingly older users also embrace this lifestyle. Why are twentysomethings overwhelmingly 24/7s? They've never known a business world without cell phones. Even if they have a hardline at home, it's become like that exercise machine buried in the closet: they don't use it. Many of their business contacts and all their friends are 24/7s. Texting is as natural to them as shaking hands was to another generation. Some think nothing of carrying more than one cell: one for international, another for domestic.

With the level of intimacy 24/7s enjoy with friends, both business and personal, they have a strikingly open attitude about interruptions. It's no big deal to be in the middle of a face-to-face conversation in the office and take a cell call without any apology or explanation. To them, the incoming caller just walked up, and they find it perfectly natural to start talking to him. The 24/7 doesn't even consider it rude to put his face-up meeting on hold. The 24/7 tests corporate boundaries. He may drop out of a meeting to take a call, or even take the call right in the room. Entire companies are becoming 24/7s, communicating with their employees via widecast text messages or calling them at all hours. In 24/7 companies, the face-to-face defers to the cell call. Old Farts don't survive, and Adopters only stand a chance if they change their mojo in time.

Yes, the 24/7 revolution is upon us. It's not just Silicon

Valley or New York or Bangalore. Companies and communities are unable to resist the insatiable desire for constant contact. But that doesn't mean it doesn't need lots of management. We aren't just talking about time. We're talking about calls with people, many of whom you'd rather not have to deal with – at least on their terms. So why do you want to take their calls? This isn't about friends or even business friends. These are the people you can't even stand exchanging e-mails with.

In other words, the really "on" 24/7 knows how to turn off. No more sugarcoating it. This is a people question. It's smarter – in a business sense – not to answer everybody's calls. To not always be available. To not be too easy. Even if the minutes are cheap, your time isn't. So where does the "on" 24/7 go? To a place and attitude where his cell becomes secretary, admin, attaché, aide-de-camp.

BY THE NUMBERS

The Pew Research Center examined how people are using their mobile technology. The numbers make clear how much farther into the future the 24/7s are running ahead of the Adopters and the Old Farts.

	24/7s	Adopters	Old Farts
Send or receive text messages	85	65	38
Access the Internet	31	22	10
Send or receive e-mail	28	21	12
Send or receive instant messages	26	18	11

(Based on a sample of 2,054 adult Americans; all figures are percentages.)

HANG UP!

Cell-phone companies are in the business of selling addiction. Every few months, they tempt us with the newest devices, services, and features – countless ways for us to integrate our cell usage with work life. Not unlike a heroin dealer advising schoolchildren how to safely handle needles. When our cells ring, we answer. When we're driving. Crossing the street. Or brainstorming with a colleague. Yes, you can mute the ringer. You can set your phone to vibrate. You can check the caller ID. And you can just turn the damn thing off. Most of us, most days, ignore these options 98.2 percent of the time.

You're in the middle of something that demands concentration or creativity. The phone rings and you foolishly grab it. Don't you hate yourself? By the time you've clicked off, your train of thought has leaped the tracks, tumbled down the embankment, and landed in a smoking ruin at the bottom of the ravine.

THE UNCALL

Whatever you do, don't increase the global interruption crisis. Thankfully, technology is helping you become part of the solution instead of part of the problem.

There's now a service that enables us to phone people and never have to hear or fear another voice. In the pre-mobile days, if you wanted to miss reaching someone, you could gamble on him either being out to lunch or home for the day. Now there's a sure bet.

The first of these services was aptly named Slydial, permitting you to dial someone's cell and skip straight to voice mail. People now have another means of dumping their latest botched hookup. The experts predict the technology will catch on in corporations. James Katz, head of mobile-communications studies at Rutgers, told the *New York Times* that indirect or intentionally missed communications are often preferable. "You pretend to be communicating, when you're actually stifling communication."

Attention, Please!

"Like so many things, in small doses, continuous partial attention can be a very functional behavior. However, in large doses, it contributes to a stressful lifestyle, to operating in crisis management mode, and to a compromised ability to reflect, to make decisions, and to think creatively. . . . We are so accessible, we're inaccessible. The latest, greatest powerful technologies have contributed to our feeling increasingly powerless."

— Linda Stone, veteran of Apple and Microsoft, coiner of the phrase "continuous partial attention"

FIGHTING THE INTERRUPTERS

Every interruption begins as a *potential* interruption.

Your cell-phone call vibrates as you're sitting in a board meeting. An e-mail chimes its arrival at your desktop just as you're finally making progress on your report. There's a knock at your office door.

Interruptions lie in the eye of the beholder. If you never reacted to these events, they wouldn't even rise to the level of an interruption. But you do react. You check caller ID, click on the e-mail, or open the door. Now you're dealing with a bona fide interruption. A human interruption – whether it's face-to-face, electronic, or a voice in your ear. The more attention you give an interruption, the worse it gets.

There are six basic stages of office interruption. No matter how severe the disruption, learn how to fight back and take control of your day.

Stage 1: Potential Interrupter

Resist clicking on that e-mail, checking the caller ID, or answering the call. Just because you're in your office doesn't mean you have to answer the door or the phone. Congratulations: you've mastered Interruption Discipline. Like the star athlete who ignores the screaming fan, you are beyond interruption.

Stage 2: Interrupter Identification

So you're not perfect. You peek at your caller ID. Can't resist scanning the e-mail subject line. We forgive you for wasting these precious seconds. That's still no excuse for hitting the "reply" button. Exercise a little restraint.

Stage 3: The Click

Click. You've answered the phone, opened the e-mail, unlocked the door. It's too late: the Interrupter has been engaged. Your only option now is to find out just how bad the interruption is going to get.

Stage 4: Interruptus Minorus

Just a slight disruption. The time it takes while you leave a caller on hold to take care of an interruption.

Or the seconds it takes to bang out a one-line e-mail response to solve a crisis.

Stage 5: Interruptus Maximus

A major pain. One that's going to demand enough of your attention that you might as well forget about what you were working on. You're going to have to start all over.

Stage 6: The Recovery

The Recovery is the amount of time it takes you to get back on task, regaining original focus and concentration.

As you develop your interruption strategies and skills, it's important to recognize the person pressing in.

- ▶ **Welcome Interrupters** can be diverting or useful – rare souls who help you get your work done faster or better.
- ▶ **Chronic Interrupters** need to be dealt with quickly to keep office life from turning sour.
- ▶ **Inside Interrupters** can be especially tough to skirt, whether they are the boss or the accountant.
- ▶ **Outside Interrupters** can really bludgeon your day. Pissed-off clients and angry customers are especially tricky to dodge.
- ▶ **Mystery Interrupters** are the wild card, the people you don't know, even if they are in your company.

Some simple overall strategies will help cut down on the negative impact Interrupters have on you and your busy day.

Whenever possible, cut your Interrupters off at the pass.

Most interruptions create a wave that throws you off balance. Instead, surf your waves in discrete sections of your day. Return most of your calls between four and five. Answer your e-mails when you first get back from lunch. Manage your hate by slicing the intrusions into bite-size chunks. Taking control of the interruptions makes them less disruptive.

Practicing Interruption Discipline requires closing real and virtual doors. Don't expect to become a master overnight. We all slip up. Forget to turn off the phone. Impulsively click on an e-mail. Before you know it, you've engaged the Interrupter.

CRAP YAK

"Today, the degradation of the inner life is symbolized by the fact that the only place sacred from interruption is the private toilet."

— LEWIS MUMFORD, HISTORIAN OF TECHNOLOGY AND SCIENCE
(1895–1990)

In some companies, the last bastion of privacy is the bathroom. Or used to be. Then some jerk walks in, yakking on his cell. It's hard not to feel violated. Some things shouldn't be shared.

There's always been something primitive yet awkward about guys standing at a row of urinals. Especially if one of them decides to strike up a conversation. But throw a dude on a cell phone in the mix, and it gets very uncomfortable: how quiet do you have to be because numbnuts is on a call? This maddening behavior isn't limited to the men's room. One woman executive we spoke to takes a proactive stance.

When a cell blabber invades her bathroom peace and quiet, "I flush and flush and flush," she says, laughing. We welcome her healthy approach. We're not opposed to generating other loud noises or yelling from a stall, "Who took the toilet paper?"

To those misguided souls who look upon toilet time as an opportunity to catch up on calls and e-mail, we have a message: Some places should be off-limits. Can it!

WHAT THE HELL DO THEY WANT?

There are three main reasons anyone is likely to call or e-mail: to get information, give information, or get you to do something. And in many large American corporations, there is a fourth: thousands of managers send blanket e-mails to cover their asses.

We all love those businesspeople who call right up, get to the point, and ask for exactly what they want. Instead, what usually happens is the NEP – Needless Exchange of Pleasantries – between people who could care less: "So nice to meet you . . . over the phone." This only ratchets up the People Hating.

Consider making your calls short. Then make them shorter. Where sixty seconds seems brief, consider twenty – then shoot for fifteen.

Brevity doesn't mean you have to be rude. Just brief. Unlike in a courtroom, there's no penalty for leading questions. Politely push to the close. You're respecting people's time by keeping things short and to the point. It does require more verbal dexterity. Which comes with practice. Ironically, far from being viewed as a curmudgeon, a fine practitioner of the short call is appreciated.

Conversely, when people call to tell you things, talk less. They'll tell you faster. The more skilled you become at the silence-and-gentle-prodding routine, the sooner they'll be trained to know that you're a "good listener." They'll also know that your time is valuable. And limited. Terminate the call by repeating the last bit of information they gave: that way, they'll know that you heard them.

Running interference is a full-time gig. We're all in a fight against the tide of e-mail, phone calls, and meetings that overwhelm our day. But pushing back or sneaking out the side door is getting harder by the minute. The smarter you get at handling interruptions, the easier it becomes to slash the number of people you have to deal with on a daily basis.

And that's enough to put a smile on the face of the most serious People Hater.

8. Off My Plate

"I'm spinning too many plates."

"You ready to step up to the plate?"

"My plate's already pretty full."

Plate analogies figure prominently in the business world. Maybe it's because everyone's plates are always filling up so fast that we're forever trying to push stuff off them. Work is the meal, and so many of the side dishes are being pressed upon us that we sometimes have trouble recognizing the main course.

As you make your way through the heaving, groaning smorgasbord that is work, the trick is to push off the things that choke your time and energy, while heaping on the nourishment and treats that drive your career and feed your curiosity.

Expert plate clearers are adept at scraping off their plates regardless of who they are, no matter what level of success they've attained. There's a lot to be learned from their techniques.

CEOs and top executives already know how critical it is to keep their agendas uncluttered. The lucky ones have assistants to organize every ten-minute block of their day. Run interference when an unplanned visit might throw things out of whack. Cut short meetings. Gently urge their boss on to his next appointment. When curveballs threaten the routine, that's when the savvy Soloist initiates one of the Three Ds: Delegate, Delay or Deny – the watchwords of the plate master.

DELEGATE

Delegating is passing off the baton to someone trustworthy. The last thing you want to do is push someone and his issue off your plate with the expectation it will be handled, only to have it come back to bite you in the ass. Delegating is tricky when you don't have an assistant whose responsibilities include backing you up. This is where cultivating an office ally pays – someone who will help lighten your load in exchange for you doing the same. Just be sure that in this tit for tat you aren't the one stuck with all the tat.

DELAY

The Delay is about balancing someone's demand on your time or attention against your need for sanity. Lawyers can teach us a lot on this subject. They're frequently in the position of being hated by the general population, not to mention their clients. And the clients want everything yesterday. A great tactic for slowing down clients or customers running at breakneck pace is voiced by a partner we interviewed at a medium-size San Francisco law firm. On Monday, it never fails that he'll get a request to turn something around in a day. His response is always the same: pick up the phone. This conversation will not be aided by e-mail. He tells the client that he's swamped. He lets that statement sink in. As he puts it, that little pause creates the basis for the punch line: "I'll try to get it to you by Wednesday."

It's all about how you phrase the Delay. Set reasonable expectations. Do it correctly, and the client is happy you're willing to go the extra mile.

Once you've mastered the Delay, you can use it to remain in control, no matter what the day serves up. "Even if I don't have a lot of shit on my desk, I'm swamped to every client," says the lawyer, sounding like, well, a lawyer.

No matter who wants something in a hurry, whether it's clients, bosses, or coworkers, the key is to always meet or beat the expectations you set. Find out the real deadline and then be reasonable and come through. "I'll probably beat that self-imposed deadline," says the lawyer. "And now everybody's happy."

DENY

"No" is often the most effective weapon in the arsenal of the Three Ds. Nothing can shut someone down faster than a flat-out denial. Used from Hollywood to Wall Street, from the inner offices of power brokers to power players, the Power of No not only commands respect, but can actually increase your core value. Movie stars and athletes say no to up their pay. If a producer truly wants Brad Pitt to star in his new film, what will he do when the star's agent rejects the original offer with a simple "No"? He'll offer more. And the Power of No will be used until Mr. Pitt gets what he wants.

SMART PLATE CLEARING

Why should you be any different from these highly successful men and women?

Well, to begin with, few of us have agents or admins. Many of us have to do our own heavy clearing. And great plate clearers avoid lying at all costs. It's not only wrong; it catches up with you and ends up piling a lot more crap on your plate.

We're big advocates of the smart use of the delayed or muted response. It's a far more sustainable strategy. The key is to say as little as possible – without generating too much hate. One manager we spoke to explained how his boss never jumps into most group e-mails. His technique is to wait until the issue truly demands his attention – or becomes unimportant and drifts away. Think of your day as a river. The secret is knowing what you can ignore or gently paddle around. Most of those ripples in the river or branches hanging over the water won't impede your progress. It's the rapids and rocks jutting up that demand your attention.

There are limits to this approach. Done too often and too crudely, the Delay can morph into the Non-Response, a popular dodge that has recently spread widely throughout the business world. We'll tackle the Non-Response in detail in a minute, but suffice to say that excessive non-responding can muster a lot of needless hate. And just because everybody else is doing it is no reason you should hop on the bandwagon.

The best practitioners of the Off My Plate phenomenon are so subtle that people don't realize they've been pushed off. We believe in that gentler, kinder push. Not quite a shove. More like a firm nudge.

Smart plate clearing requires psychology. Our friend Hollywood producer Harvey Myman is that true rarity in show business: a genuinely nice guy. He truly hates being rude or mean to someone. Even to people who treat him badly. But Harvey, like many successful executives, is inundated with demands on his time that he can't possibly meet. Every week, he's sent dozens of scripts that he can't possibly read. Every week, a few writers or agents push too hard. Harvey has come up with a brilliant, sincere line to back them off: "Having me read it wouldn't be the best use of *your* time." Why does this work? It's being honest. And by reversing the expected logic, Harvey is gently telling people that they would be wise to push elsewhere.

Another nice guy in Hollywood happens to be Harvey's brother, Bob Myman. What's weird is that he's still nice even though he's in L.A. and he's consistently on the Fifty Most Powerful Hollywood Attorneys lists. Time is at a premium, but Bob has refined his plate-clearing chops. When you send him an e-mail, rather than getting a note back from his assistant, you'll get a personal e-mail back before the end of the day. Chances are it's just a word or two – usually all in lowercase letters and simply signed "Bob," so you know it came from him. And the answer will be useful, even if it's just to say he'll talk to you about the matter later.

Compare that to what you're likely to get from the other

major players in Hollywood or business. There's the Assistant's Response, which often feels like a dodge and rarely resolves the issue. Worse is the Assistant's Assistant's Response – universally useless. But the most irksome response of all is not the Assistant's or even the Assistant's Assistant's Response. It's no response at all.

> *"The worst sin toward our fellow creatures is not to hate them, but to be indifferent to them; that's the essence of inhumanity."*
>
> — GEORGE BERNARD SHAW

Many corporate people are interrupted so often on so many different levels that they've adopted the Non-Response as a universal defense mechanism. It comes in many flavors. The first is silence. They don't respond to your e-mail or phone messages. Zilch. It's not overtly hostile, but there's nothing you can do with it.

We're in the midst of a global meltdown. E-mail and voice-mail overload have ruined our manners. We're so inundated that even when we ask people to send us stuff – reports, files, proofs – we don't even take the time to type or call back "Thanks" or "Got it." This is like not saying "Thank you" for a gift. It's one of the most visible signs of civilization's decline. And manners are quickly being forgotten, along with holding the door for old ladies, not taking up two parking spaces, and saying "Gesundheit" after someone sneezes. Remember a little something called business etiquette?

The Non-Response is the most common way someone in a company may blunt your progress. He may be a Stop Sign or a Sheeple or just too busy or rude to bother. But by his not returning your e-mail or messages, your progress is effectively stopped. He can later claim grade-school-style excuses: "Our server's been down!" "I didn't get your message!" "I was caught in a bear trap!"

Signs that you're getting a Non-Response:

▶ **The Pseudo-Response**
Most often a terse one-line e-mail: "Got it!"

▶ **The Deflected Non-Response**
Though they appear to answer your e-mail, they deftly avoid answering your question. You're unlikely to squeeze anything more out of them until they need something from you.

▶ **The Assisted Non-Response**
The front man calls you back – and tells you nothing. It's the trusty cover for the slippery Non-Responder. When pressed, the boss will typically feign ignorance of your call and blame his assistant.

▶ **The Courtesy Non-Response**
Wrapped in champagne, fruit baskets, or candy, along with a handwritten note promising great things. Popular in massive corporations and Hollywood. What's missing? Any real communication channel. When you call, they're not in, and the assistant takes your messages and e-mails, leaving you stuck with the flat bubbly and rotten fruit.

▶ **The Smoothy Non-Response**
You don't even know you've been non-responded to. He's so slick that it feels as though he's on your side, advocating your causes, and yet it isn't until you've hung up the phone or let the e-mail sink in that you realize nothing has happened.

► **The WTF Non-Response**

You're made to feel as though you're intruding, when all you want is a straight answer for something they said they'd be happy to provide. You call for the budget numbers they promised you last week, but when they finally answer, you get a belligerent, "I told you I'd get those numbers to you when they're ready!"

HOW TO RESPOND TO THE NON-RESPONSE

There's really only one strategy to outflank a Non-Responder: work a different communication medium. Walk down the hall. Forget trying another e-mail or recording another message. There's no point. And when someone is truly brushing you off, the most practical alternative is often to open another door. Search out someone else to resolve your issue or provide the support you need. When you need the Non-Responder's help on other projects, consider giving him one final chance in a voice-mail or e-mail message: "I've asked for your support on this over the past week. I'm out of time. I'm taking this to someone who can help me."

Sending countless e-mails and leaving endless messages is like shouting into a canyon: all you're likely to hear is the echo of your own voice. Non-Responders require more finesse and creativity. Less is more. It can be as simple as a clever subject line in your next e-mail. Or a cryptic phone message. Non-respond the Non-Responder. Leave out enough to spark his curiosity and fear:

"We're moving the meeting."

"The client changed his mind."

A vice president of production told us a trick that worked wonders with a Chronic Non-Responder. He sent the Non-Responder an interoffice fax with a cover sheet in a color that he knew would garner attention: fuchsia. The document was blunt: approval or comment was required within a day or the team would move on without him. The combination of the striking paper choice and the ultimatum broke through the gray routine. The Non-Responder laughed – and, most important, responded.

The same VP has staged an even more direct approach: the impromptu "Non-Response intervention." He marched an entire project team into a Non-Responder office to force an answer.

Vernon Hurd, the DG FastChannel systems analyst whose interactions are mostly by phone and e-mail from his home in Kansas to the office he's assigned to in Texas, says he's often challenged by the Non-Responder. He doesn't have the option of heading down the hall and smacking him around. He hits "perpetual" Non-Responders with a phone-and-e-mail combo. He lets them know in a direct phone message what he needs and why – and then drops a hard deadline. His close is what gets their attention. He says, "If I don't hear back from you by such-and-such a time, I'll just go ahead and call your supervisor and see if there is someone they'd rather I use as a resource." He follows the same strategy with e-mail, suggesting that he'll go to a superior for an alternate resource. It's a power play that works. Says Hurd: "I've found that the simple mention of asking their boss for another resource inevitably gets a response."

The PR director of a popular resort prefers an overly inclusive approach for people she intuits may be non-responsive. She reaches out, saying she's happy to communicate and work with them, giving them the choice of regularly scheduled meetings, e-mail updates, or drop-ins at their office. By actively seeking out how they prefer to interact, she says, "they feel slightly more obligated to reply to you since they know you respect their work flow and style." Case in point: the hotel's executive chef prefers quick one-on-one meetings that run down a to-do list. "Try to coordinate anything via e-mail with him, and it just leads to frustration," says the PR director. "That's not how he works."

The retro fax technique we mentioned above works astonishingly well – largely because no one in this age of e-mail expects it. Sending someone a simple fax asking for a callback grabs people's attention.

WHEN THINGS GO SOUTH

The Chronic Non-Responder has an ace up his sleeve. When you finally manage to push through the deflecting e-mails and chatter-face calls and confront your target, beware. He often acts like an angry mama grizzly bear protecting her young. But here the young may be you, your project, your team, or your company. You're often caught off guard. The Chronic Non-Responder abruptly turns emotional, even angry. It's as if he suddenly cranked up the volume. As if noise will somehow make you and your issue go away. The wisdom of your inquiry will be challenged. Troublemaker! Your request rocks the boat and threatens the Way Things Are Done.

DO NOT DISTURB

In case you haven't noticed, it has become acceptable, indeed fashionable, to be unreachable. If the Soloist in you desperately needs alone time, we suggest taking a page from Neal Stephenson, famed sci-fi author of *Snow Crash* and other best sellers. Until you write your Great American Novel, you may not be able to close the door to intruders full-time. But consider holding up the Do Not Disturb sign for a day or a week — especially when under a project deadline (remember that thing called work). The key is to make it abundantly clear that you are not open for unsolicited e-mail, text messages, voice mail, or other sundry incursions on your humanity. As Stephenson once put it so clearly on the Internet:

The purpose of this web page is to help me focus all of my attention on productive activity. Three strategies are used:

> ▷ **explicit discouragement**
> *Persons who wish to interfere with my concentration are politely requested not to do so, and warned that I don't answer e-mail.*
> ▷ **FAQs**
> *Persons who wish to ask me questions are encouraged to look for the answers here on this page.*
> ▷ **redirection**
> *Persons wishing to make business proposals are aimed in the direction of my agents.*

If you're unfamiliar with Chronic Non-Responders, this sudden outburst will shock. That's what they're counting on – the element of surprise. Knocking you off balance. Then blustering forward with illogical arguments.

The first step is to do absolutely nothing.

A few seconds of silence. Let the air out of the balloon. You're just trying to get a project done, a product shipped, payment made.

Don't take any of it personally. Acknowledge the anger but don't get angry yourself. Calmly move to bring the issue back to business. It's kind of like the old marriage-counseling saw: it takes two to argue.

Simplify the issue into bite-size pieces. And take the emotion off the table. Because chances are the emotions you're seeing are phony. Most Chronics have learned that posing emotionally generally gets them what they want. The key is for you to stick to the two or three tangibles that you need: a commitment, action, or authorization. Leave no wiggle room for the Chronic, and she quickly gets the message: playing loud and rough failed. Even if this Chronic is the worst possible belligerent Bulldozer, your calm and deliberate approach will gradually prove effective. Over time, the Chronic will discover that you're not like the other boys and girls.

Congratulations! You've pulled off something amazing: you've actually gotten a Chronic Non-Responder to respond.

PRACTICING PORTION CONTROL

Some problems you'll be able to scrape off your plate onto someone else's. Others can be flipped back to the person who served them to you. But the majority of stuff that gets pushed off has a tendency to crawl back unless you take definitive action. If you're a messy eater – indiscriminately shoving things off your plate – you're likely to end up hip deep in table scraps: incomplete projects, unresolved issues, conflicting schedules.

As with a well-planned diet, decide in advance how much your plate can comfortably hold. Or think of your plate as an old-fashioned TV dinner or a Japanese bento box: with a compartment to hold each dish. The compartments separate the dishes and determine how much of each dish is served. The main course always gets the most space, and once the spaces are filled, they can't hold any more.

Don't overload. Make it a point to clear out a compartment before taking on more. During crazy, hectic times when you absolutely have to grab an extra dish or two, make sure you work harder to clear your plate.

To paraphrase Ella Williams, if you're going to bite off more than you can chew, you better start chewing faster.

9. The Disrupters

We began this book with the naive idea that there were ten archetypes wreaking havoc across corporate America. As we talked to more and more men and women in corporations, reality struck. There are a lot more than ten kinds of disruptive people. Our challenge became how to keep the list from becoming unwieldy. In the end, we decided to stick with our trusty ten, and start a second list.

The Disrupters. They don't pose danger on the same scale as the Ten Least Wanted. They won't take your job, steal your ideas, or drive you to turn in your stapler and call it quits. That doesn't mean you want them to be your next-door cubie. The Disrupters are subtle and brutal all at once: we think of them as the workplace equivalent of Chinese water torture, or perhaps as Death by a Thousand Cuts. Slow and insidious, over the course of hours or days or weeks, any one Disrupter can shove you over the brink.

Unlike with the Ten Least Wanted, there are few foolproof techniques to combat the Disrupters other than frequent coffee and bathroom breaks – or that business trip to Cleveland. Some might say that the Disrupters can be overcome by adopting meditation and relaxation techniques. Light a candle. Burn some incense. Play Mongolian monk throat-song chants. Are you kidding? This is the office. Even if you could get away with having all that crap in your cube, it won't do a damn bit of good.

We've noticed that office etiquette experts advise a five-step battle plan, which often includes readying yourself for conflict and recruiting a fellow anti-Disrupter. This is reasonable, straightforward advice. The trouble comes if you confuse dealing with a Disrupter with healing a Disrupter. Jennifer Gruenemay of LifeScript, the health and lifestyle site, also recommends that you "lend a helping hand." Echoing the prevailing school of office nice, Gruenemay says you should be sensitive to the "troubled soul" and look beyond the negative behavior. "Bullying is a shield to protect what's vulnerable and fragile inside," she asserts. "Break down that barrier and you may find someone who could use a friend."

Or not.

Social work doesn't fall within your job description.

We prefer another of Gruenemay's tips: move on. When confronted by a Disrupter, the first rule of thumb is to simply minimize contact. And sometimes your best defense is just a good healthy laugh in the face of people who, despite your best intentions, you may not be able to change.

Here, then, are the Disrupters.

▶ **Unprepared**

Never brings a pen to meetings. Forgot to read the memo. It's not just that he's an occasional dimwit – we all have those moments when we suffer a mind leak. The problem is that Unprepared always seems to want to borrow *your* pen.

▶ **Cud**

That crud a cow works over in its massive mandible all day long – remind you of anyone? Like maybe your office's endless eater? It's bad enough that he eats more than the Three Little Pigs, but you are doomed to suffer the horrid accompanying sound effects.

▶ **Bad Comedian**

Jokes spew from him like bees from a broken hive. The stand-up routine around the watercooler. E-mails. They're lame. Tasteless. A few are funny. Don't laugh: you're only encouraging him. There's no easy out – except maybe the fire escape.

> Gossiping, not doing your share of office kitchen dishes, wearing bad perfume and being loud are among the top offenses in a pet peeves–themed survey of 2,429 adults.
>
> — Randstad, human resources firm

▶ **Hyena**

Laughs at everything. YouTube videos. Cute cat pictures. Fart sounds. It doesn't matter. If it happens on

TOP ELEVEN OFFICE PEEVES

Sometimes Disrupters aren't the people: it's their behavior. Which means we can all be guilty of doing things that piss people off from time to time and not even be aware of it. Thanks to a survey by Ceridian LifeWorks, we have a definitive list of the behaviors that more often than not rankle the rank and file. As you peruse the list, find the behaviors you're guilty of — and knock it off.

1. Loud talking.*
2. Annoying cell-phone ringtones.
3. Talking on speakerphone.
4. Lousy manners.
5. Foul personal hygiene.
6. Constant moaning.
7. Not doing office dishes.
8. Blowing off a task.
9. Singing along to the radio.
10. Walking too heavily.
11. Shaking hands like a fish.

*Loud Talkers are the most annoying office miscreants, according to a recent study of 2,318 people, followed closely by people with stupid ringtones and those who yap on speakerphone.

— Harris Interactive and Randstad

the face of the earth, it's hilarious to the Hyena. Worst of all, he often wants to share the hilarity. There's no escaping the guffaws, chuckles, and roars of laughter meant to drag you into his cube to ask, "What's so funny?"

▶ **Yackety Yak**

His constant chattering gives other people license to talk, and then the volume ratchets up exponentially. You can cough. Clear your throat. Nothing short of a brazen "Shut up!" clamps Yackety Yak's voice hole.

▶ **Swipe**

That sticky-fingered culprit who helps himself to things with every intention of never returning them. Staplers, pencils, notepads – stuff from your desk vanishes. Even when you've deduced the identity of the Swipe, you still can't figure out what happened to the missing items. And Swipe never has anything worth swiping in return.

▶ **Buzz Saw**

Loves to pepper his office jawing with buzzwords, heaping the latest terms and clichés on top of the old. A slang compost heap composed of "Shoot you an e-mail," "Touch base," "Circle back," "Let's take that one offline," "Mission critical," "Raising the bar," and "Drill down." It's all just office filler. Pinned to the dingy carpet, Buzz Saw probably couldn't explain half of his spewage. We're sure you'd agree "110 percent."

▶ **Hard-On**

Formerly known as male chauvinist pigs, Hard-Ons were beaten off in the 1970s by the Feministas. The Hard-Ons stayed under wraps but kept rubbing up against temptation. But there's no keeping a bad man down, and businesswomen continue to find themselves harassed.

▶ **Space Invader**

Crashes your personal space. If he's close enough to strangle you, he's too close. If you can make out the rotting molars and pitted acne and are overcome by the halitosis, he's *way* too close.

▶ **Sound FX**

Everyone has a Clicker, the frustrated musician who must click one object on his desk against another, like a pen against a coffee mug. Slurper can't seem to drink anything – coffee, water, soup – without that obtrusive sucking noise. And Squeaker's desk chair squeals every time he moves.

▶ **Vulture**

Crashes any and all meetings that feature food. Many of these corporate parasites are such gluttons that they'll gladly stomach an extra meeting that has nothing to do with their work for an impromptu feed.

▶ **Play by Play**

Can't make a move without broadcasting it: "I'm going to refill the toner!" "I'm off to the Mexican place for lunch!" "I'll be in the bathroom if anyone calls!" These phrases are rhetorical, you quickly learn – no response is expected. And there's no way to stop the announcements.

▶ **Annoyance**

Some office types aren't genuinely disruptive. They just manage to get on what nerves we have left. They may not be loud or intrusive but still fray the cords of our basic office fibers. Annoyances are more like the distraction of a car crash. We shouldn't look, but we can't help ourselves. Sometimes there's no logical reason why the Annoyances should bother us; they just do. Job search giant Monster.com notes that just walking like an elephant is enough to bother us, not to mention those spineless office creatures who shake hands like a fish and avoid eye contact.

Indian office workers detest what the Indian portal Oneindia calls "Pod pong," people who "marinate themselves in perfumes," or the "Snot funny," sick workers who lack the decency to keep their noxious germs home.

The Brits, who, after all, coined the brilliant phrase "Piss off" and brought us the TV show *The Office,* deserve credit for assuming worldwide leadership in discerning the human workplace failings that drive us to distraction. The British study – and take seriously – office annoyances more than perhaps any other nation. As fans of both British and American versions of *The Office* know, there's a distinct difference in British workplace sensibilities. Brits have special disdain for those who work either too hard or too little. They loathe losers. Check out the eleven most despised personality types in Britain, compiled by a survey of two thousand workers conducted by 72 Point, a major public-relations firm.

1. The Brown Noser.
2. The No. 1.
3. The Corporate Speaker.
4. The Malingerer.
5. The Clock Watcher.
6. The Social Secretary.
7. The Letch.
8. The Toilet Weeper.
9. The Mum.

10. The Dieter.
11. The Love Flop.

Translation note: The No. 1 is that person the British find especially irritating, the one who manages to do his work better, faster, sooner, and cheaper. "Malingerer" is Britspeak for slacker. The Mum makes tea or coffee and knows the location of the first-aid kit. The Love Flop . . . you know what that is.

10. Fool the Rules

"Any fool can make a rule, and any fool will mind it."
— Henry David Thoreau

When you first started work, chances are human resources handed you a binder filled with The Rules: Dress code. Work hours. What you can't have in your cube. On and on and on go The Rules. You flipped through it once, lingered over the regulations pertaining to sexual harassment, then put it away. Now it's just taking up space on the one over-crowded shelf you're allotted. And you'd better not throw it out in case someone calls you on The Rules.

Society couldn't function without rules. And without staying within certain parameters, companies couldn't succeed. The opportunity lies in the fact that many rules have more leeway than most would assume. Which means, for the discerning Soloist, there are loopholes that can be played to your advantage.

Any great jazz musician who improvises brilliantly will tell you that there's a secret to be able to play crazy notes and make it sound like music. You've got to know how to play by the rules first in order to break them properly.

Being a Soloist is all about fooling the rules. The best way to shave off Solocrafting time usually means bending, twisting, or breaking one rule or another. "Rules were meant to separate people. There are the people who see rules as a ceiling or an endpoint," says website architect Shane Elliott. "And the people who see rules as a guideline or a starting point." He regards those who take the rules at face value as Sheeple, while those who hate having the rules shoved in their faces are clearly Soloists.

The problem is that many corporate rules don't do much of anything except cloud normal human relations. Consider the laws against sexual harassment. Necessary. Politically correct. Who could argue with that? But we interviewed women who feel that the hypersensitivity around nearly all male-female interaction in the office has left them uncertain of the most ordinary situations. "The rules against sexual harassment have messed things up," says one young woman who worked in marketing at a large company. "Anything you do you have to watch. If some guy cuts in front of you to get a cup of coffee, somebody will say, 'It should be ladies first.' And then somebody else will say, 'That's sexist.'"

Another problem in large organizations is that there are officials who call the fouls. "The head of HR is like the big bad principal – the ruler of The Rules," continues the marketing woman. "We had three key people in HR. One was

Happy Face, the cheerleader, always talking about teams. Another was the Grim Reaper, the one who fired you. And the third was the Rules Person."

Putting human resources in charge of the rules is a bit like what's happened to sports in America: lots of rules and lots of cheating. Studies show that imposing behavior doesn't work much better than hitting children used to for parents or teachers – or for children. It's no different in an even bigger organization where the rules often seem arbitrarily designed to keep you from doing your job – or at least feeling good about it.

REWRITING THE UNWRITTEN RULES

Some of the most sacrosanct rules in companies are the unwritten ones. You often only find out about them when you get dinged or, ironically, "written up." Human resources won't tell you about them. They're not in the binder with all the other rules 'n' regs. Little things like "Nobody leaves before the boss." "Only Mrs. Hadley can order office supplies." "Last one to leave the conference room has to clean up."

The trouble with unwritten rules is that, without specific language to keep them nailed in place, they tend to shift. When Jerry was the marketing and communications director of a Boston-based oil and gas company, he fell prey to the unwritten rules of a fluctuating Spreadsheet: "The place had a micromanager boss, but he was very inconsistent." The Spreadsheet kept changing the rules. Jerry would let him know the rising total of funding needed to pull off their marketing strategy. At each juncture where cash was needed, the boss would say, "Okay, that might be doable." Taking that as a go, "I'd commit, and then once everything was really rolling, he'd come back and ask why I was spending all this money."

> *"Rules are mostly made to be broken and are too often for the lazy to hide behind."*
> — GENERAL DOUGLAS MACARTHUR

Create your own unwritten rules to outwit the written ones. Clorox, for example, is a company that believes in a rigid business approach. "There's a process for everything," Theresa, a former associate brand manager, told us. "It's written down somewhere. When you ask why, the answer is often, 'That's just the way we do it.'"

When things turn impersonal, it's time to make it more personal. "I got around it by establishing strong relationships with people," says Theresa. "Sometimes it's playing dumb about the process. And only doing it [getting around the rules] when you know where you're headed and your ducks are all aligned." There was no policy in place for when Theresa wanted to start working from home one day a week – a move that would give her a chance to really get some traction on difficult projects. With no written policy about it, "I just carefully made sure I didn't have any meetings lined up that day."

As for the rest of the week, Theresa was religious about leaving at quitting time. Though she had numerous colleagues who worked until ten at night, she didn't let them stop her from going out the door before dusk. "People definitely noticed me trying to get out at a decent hour," she says. "I probably worked fewer hours than the other brand people, but I was among the highest performers." Even during some evenings when she'd work at home, Theresa took pains not to let people know what she was up to. Sometimes Sheeple send e-mails from home late at night to show how hard they're working. She took the opposite tack, keeping her work communications strictly during normal work hours.

By creating her own unwritten rules in the face of the Clorox bureaucracy, Theresa was able to create an image of herself as the corporate poster child, someone able to do the impossible: get all her allotted work done between the hours of 9:00 a.m. and 5:00 p.m.

Carl Haney, whom we met before, began his career in Venezuela working for Procter & Gamble, a great opportunity except that during his first decade for the firm he was paid in the weak local currency. One day in 1992, while flying back from the London offices of P&G to Caracas, he wrote his lifetime goals on a simple organizer – five-, ten-, fifteen-, and twenty-year plans. Haney loved the firm, but the bolivars weren't adding up.

Shortly thereafter, a newly emboldened Haney wrote "the bloody letter," as he recalls it, a one-page affair to the president of the firm's research division. He calmly listed his lifetime cumulative compensation for his ten years of service, said he enjoyed his work and respected the firm, but had to consider other alternatives.

Haney heard nothing for months, but instead of seeking out other opportunities, he kept working just as hard as before. Then, out of the blue, he received a company stock option. There was no explanation, no communication from the firm. The value of the grant was nearly his entire salary for the previous decade. Haney no longer felt he'd been financially undervalued by being paid in foreign currency.

"That one event made up for the previous decade," says Haney. "It put me on a comparable pay scale."

And it guaranteed that he remained a loyal Stay-Put Soloist.

NO MORE RULES

If you're worried about breaking company rules, flouting standard practices, and ruffling corporate feathers, fear not. American corporations are perfectly happy to pull all the rules right out from under you. Yes, that's right. Game over. You're fired. Bye-bye. Half the time the firing has nothing to do with your performance. A corporate raider swoops in and carves up the company like a turkey – and you're the giblets. The company needs to show a profit, and sales have been slack, so it decides to lighten the load. Never mind that you're one of the people actually doing something.

Worst of all, they've learned how to do it without getting their own hands dirty. *Inc.* magazine recently reported that more and more corporations are outsourcing the most distasteful part of employment: the day you're told to cram all your personal effects in a single box, to then be escorted off the premises by a $9-an-hour security guard. Why go to the outside? "There can be an emotional barrier that neither person can get past," says J. P. Magill, cofounder of a "terminator" – a company that specializes in lowering the boom for others. "At that point, you need to isolate the organization from the termination."

Not that companies are having any problem quickly distancing themselves from their ever-so-recently dedicated and loyal workers. *Inc.* reported that when human-resources company PeopleSoft was gobbled up by Oracle, five thousand Saturdays were disrupted by the arrival of overnight packages informing employees that they were either the lucky winners of a new job or else the luckless recipients of a severance package. RadioShack took a step closer toward the impersonal by sacking four hundred employees by *e-mail.* While the company certainly saved money on the FedEx charges, perhaps it should have paid a writer to sugarcoat the dropping of the ax. Incredibly, the e-mail read, "The work-force reduction notification is currently in progress. Unfortunately, your position is one that has been eliminated."

The message is clear. The company controls the rules and can change them anytime it wants. Sounds like a good rationale for a healthy irreverence for The Rules.

CREATIVITY KNOWS NO RULES

Psychologists, behaviorists, and researchers have investigated the tricky nature of inspiration and creativity. Studies of children reveal that most adult approaches to creativity stink. Teachers who offer prizes or rewards for artwork, story writing, and other artistic pursuits end up stunting their little charges. Once the reward – a ribbon, a gold star, an ice-cream cone – becomes the goal, the quality of the work suffers. And over time, the kids tend to lose all interest in these endeavors.

A number of related studies have shown that intrinsic interest in a given task – something thought to be worth doing for its own sake – plummets when someone is rewarded for doing it. And the same findings hold true from childhood to adulthood. Kids rewarded for drawing are less likely to draw on their own than are their counterparts who draw for the fun of it. For instance, teens offered incentives didn't enjoy playing word games and were outperformed by teens not offered the carrot. Adult employees, praised for meeting a manager's expectations, were found to suffer a corresponding drop in motivation.

These findings are well established, and yet corporate America has largely failed to use them toward making a work environment more conducive to creativity and productivity. For instance, twenty years ago, in a study at Brandeis and Boston universities, researcher Teresa Amabile asked dozens of creative writers to pen some poetry. She split the participants into three groups. One had extrinsic reasons to write: impressing teachers, making cash, and getting into grad school. The second crew was given intrinsic reasons: the enjoyment of playing with words, the satisfaction of self-expression, et cetera. The third group was told nothing – just to write some poetry.

You can see where this is going. The group given all those external reasons to rhyme it up wrote less creatively, and the quality of their work suffered. The other two groups did much better. In other words, the rewards got in the way of creative tasks and higher-level problem solving. Said Amabile: "The more complex the activity, the more it's hurt by extrinsic reward."

American youth sports are a perfect example of this phenomenon. Millions of talented children are forced into sports labor camps (leagues) from the age of five. Studies have shown that even the best inevitably retire after seven years of intensive competition. Meaning they are finished before they've even matured.

Studies of adult professional painters – the bohemian variety – have also shown the danger of the reward effect. Experts analyzing the canvases of noted artists have discovered that the commissioned paintings are inevitably of an inferior quality. This fact is even more impressive given that commissioned artists often have greater time and resources to complete the "official" creativity.

The corporate approach is also reward based, most commonly known as "bonuses." It's a formula of financial incentives built out of one part carrot and one part stick. Many employees don't have the faintest idea of how their bonus is calculated. This may work to encourage employees to ship more boxes, but there's little evidence that it helps them come up with something interesting to put in the boxes.

The trouble with all these ulterior motives – money, peer recognition, advancement – is that they aren't *interior* motives. You know: doing things simply out of curiosity, pleasure, and a need to explore. That need that never disappears, as long as you don't try to fuel it with too many carrots and sticks. We're talking about the human condition, and the trick is not to let our natural flow be disrupted by the office condition crushing the urge to explore. Replacing creativity with a series of Stupid Office Tricks: Get the report. Find the data. Deliver the presentation. Good boy!

We began this chapter with the famous quote from Thoreau, "Any fool can make a rule, and any fool will mind it." We think the best quotation to end on comes from a man who knew how to get stuff done in spite of other people, Thomas Edison. "Hell, there are no rules here – we are trying to accomplish something."

FOUR

SPACES AND PLACES

11. Dig My Cave

"Within this cave, there is an inexhaustible treasure."
— SRI GURU GRANTH SAHIB

Man's need for a Cave is as basic as his need for food and water.

We all want a place to call our own. Funny thing about Caves: One is not enough. First we get a Home Cave, then a Work Cave. But the Caves provided by companies – cubes and offices – offer scant shelter from the forces of annoyance: the torrent of e-mails, blizzard of cell calls, and hailstorm of coworkers punishing our privacy. For hundreds of thousands in the financial world, there's not even the luxury of a cube or office. You're crammed into the great "bull pen," a forced friendly term to describe bleak desks mashed up against one another without any dividers or other shields against interminable noises, endless lame stories, and frequent nose pickings.

Get yourself a Personal Cave.

More than just a place, it's a state of being. It can be at home or in a garage, basement, garden, or café – even in the office cube. The Personal Cave begins when you take command of your cube's three partitions, office's four walls, or corner of a café. Mark off your territory. Break a rule or two.

Why is this so important? The high-tech revolution has cost too many of us our Caves. Sure, it's great to be mobile, to have everyone you need to call, text, or e-mail at the touch of your fingers. Mobility allows you to run, but you still can't hide.

You're eventually going to need a Cave. The creative cocoon that allows you to do all those things best done without interruption.

In a perfect world, your corporate cube or office would be the only other Cave you need. But then you may have already been shoved out of your office building's footprint. Roughly forty-five million Americans already telecommute at least one day a week, according to AeA (formerly Technology Association of America). Today, seven in ten Americans have offices in their homes.

Another reason for creating a Personal Cave is the trend toward increasing numbers of workers spending three or more days a week out of the office. Those workers need Caves to be productive and creative – places to Solocraft.

As we were writing this book, state and city governments were tripping over one another in rushing to institute four-day workweeks. Though the moves were often cast as smart attempts to reduce energy use in the face of global warming and erratic oil prices, nearly every governor or mayor said an equally important rationale was to improve productivity and staff morale. "It makes me a happier employee," said one state office worker in Montgomery, Alabama. "I think that shows at work."

Utah was the first state to make the shift. Governor Jon Huntsman says younger workers love the four-day workweek, and he thinks giving workers a longer weekend will increase the state's ability to attract talent.

We think this tide will wash over into business, though corporate resistance remains firm. Despite the government shift toward four-day workweeks, many companies have dug in their heels and clung to the myth that telecommuting (and shorter weeks) don't work. Numerous publications have run stories about how it can breed office envy for those not lucky enough to work from home. Here are the facts. Researchers at Penn State reviewed forty-six studies featuring nearly thirteen thousand employees and found that home workers enjoyed seven positive benefits, from increased control over their work and environment to improved productivity, career prospects, and supervisor-staff relationships. Workers covet increased independence, says lead researcher Ravi S. Gajendran. Telecommuters reported diminished stress, superior work-family balance, and higher performance ratings. What about "face time," the creaky corporate dogma that you must be at the office to excel? Contrary to those tired expectations, telecommuting damages neither your office relationships nor your career. Bosses were impressed by *out-of-sight* performance.

Few of us are lucky enough to be telecommuting. Most American workers still spend three to five days a week in a traditional office. Even if you have an office with a door, you probably can't close it for long. If you're a cube dweller, there's nowhere to hide, and experimentation is frowned upon. You can even be cited for having items poking out of your cube. Nonstandard chairs, furniture, or fixtures may be verboten. Don't even think about repainting anything beyond the standard industrial white or institutional gray. The Rules, remember? You're just the hired help, and the idea that you might have a say in improving your immediate surroundings, in making this a place you enjoy instead of hate, is about as likely today at most companies as grade-school students being given the license to remodel their classrooms.

Turns out the straitjacketed office isn't quite all it's cracked up to be. The real-estate firm Blumberg Capital Partners recently released a nationwide survey on what oppressive office buildings do to the minds and spirits of workers. Nearly half the respondents said that extreme temperatures – so cold they can barely feel their fingers, or so hot that they're dozing off – plague their office. Half complain that they toil in bland, dumpy, or stodgy buildings. One in three workers say they have either left or taken a new job largely based on the condition of the building or the amenities it offered. Four out of five say their building affects how they view their employer. A third worry their building may hurt them or make them sick. And nearly 70 percent say their productivity and motivation are directly influenced by the condition of their surroundings.

"We don't have a lot of time on this earth! We weren't meant to spend it this way. Human beings were not meant to sit in little cubicles staring at computer screens all day, filling out useless forms and listening to eight different bosses drone on about mission statements."

— PETER GIBBONS, *OFFICE SPACE*

Jerry Murphy, a New York–based organizational learning and development expert, equates office space to man's primal needs. We're all looking to be part of a village, he says. "A lot of the Soloist syndrome is a reaction to improperly designed space. 'I can't work in an open space' or 'This cubicle sucks.' Or 'I'm all alone in my office.'"

Bad designs are just the start. The corporate cube and office keep shrinking. Back in the spacious 1980s, each employee got about 227 square feet. This century, it has been hacked down to between 150 and 200 square feet. Companies have been trying to crack the employee's mental connection between nice offices and status for years. The *New York Times* wrote a few years ago about Pricewaterhouse Coopers's plans for its Manhattan offices. The giant accounting firm sounded giddy about taking "partners who now luxuriate in window offices averaging 250 square feet" and packing them like sardines into spaces half that size, with managers accustomed to 140 square feet being scrunched into just 80 – smaller than most executives' closets.

The Big Squeeze is on. Largely in the pursuit of that poorly understood cliché "innovation," companies are sticking workers into places so tiny that it's time to christen the diminutive form: the Cubelet. The corporate hard-on for group work and teamwork and crushing the individual has created a cultlike frenzy to shrink your space while companies merrily expand "teaming areas," giving you practically nowhere to hide. Ironically, several workers report that sometimes the best place to escape from the scurry is a team room outside their area. Says one executive: "With the open office environment, in order to have solo time, you need to go hide somewhere."

Companies want to encourage interaction and discourage workers from viewing the office as a status symbol. As a real-estate expert told the *New York Times,* "Space was used as a psychic form of compensation. To a large extent, that's changed."

Music Box

. . . .

How liberating can it be to escape cubedom? One executive told us that after dutifully serving two years in the cubes, she was finally granted an office. "I instantly closed the door, turned up the music, and wouldn't talk to anyone if I could help it."

Cubelets or cookie-cutter offices with glass walls are now standard. The office is no home away from home. No psychic compensation or springboard for motivation. Your Corporate Cave has been pillaged. The prime spots swallowed up by the insidious group space designers dub "neighborhood parks." You've been robbed, left with less of everything, especially what man needs in a Cave: walls, doors, and privacy.

In lieu of being able to pimp their cube, the best most can do is dot their space with strategically placed tchotchkes:

a collection of snow globes, PEZ dispensers, an auto-graphed baseball, or anything else that dimly reflects their personality. But even that hobbled strategy is under attack by officialdom.

GETTING PERSONAL

Researchers at the University of Michigan's business school recently proclaimed they had discovered a critical new business principle. The results were broadcast on National Public Radio and in dozens of newspapers. What was the crux of this brilliant study? Doodads, tchotchkes, and family photos threaten the fabric of the corporate structure. The study concluded that if more than one in five items in your office or cube is not a stapler, paper clip, rubber band, file folder, or other nineteenth-century artifact, you will be perceived as unprofessional by the Powers That Be.

Amazingly, nobody made fun of this research. Far from it. Offices across the land are rushing to enforce the "20/80 rule," carefully measuring the ratio of human to drone stuff. The business professors who orchestrated this noise actually believe you will go farther in professional America if you turn your office into a corporate mauso-leum. The following silly assertion spawned the national media frenzy: "Minor personal references in the work-place – even as a way to build personal rapport – can have a negative influence on how one is evaluated by recruiters for American companies and success in the recruitment process."

It's understandable some executives might feel com-pelled by years of corporate drudgery to maintain a degree of bare-deskedness. But the countless productive people who dream up and implement America's new products and services thrive by personalizing their work environment. Case in point: Procter & Gamble, the consumer-products giant, pays countless millions every year to IDEO, the noted hipster design-strategy firm, precisely because nearly every IDEO designer and engineer hops to the "80/20 rule": 80 percent of their workspace reflects their passions, and only 20 percent is the staplers and other office ballast. Remember Dennis Boyle, creator of the IDEO Tech Box? His corner spread is famous for the fifteen-foot structure that resembles the Eiffel Tower, not to mention the striped awning taken straight from a Paris café. Another IDEOer was revered for his collection of quirky nonperishable foods. It helps that founder David Kelley has always filled his office with fanciful touches, like neon lights and motorcycles.

There's a weird twist at play at the company. IDEOers who don't celebrate their hobbies or prototypes in their office or cube run the risk of appearing dull, if not downright unimaginative.

Clue in to the smart workers and clever companies that are constantly experimenting with workspaces that inspire. They don't measure what's "professional" versus "personal." No straitjackets here. They celebrate their life, interests, and hobbies in their Caves.

> Telework arrangements are the best hiring incentive, according to one-third of chief financial officers.
>
> — Technology Association of America
> 2008 study of 1,400 CFOs

DEAD ZONES

Cool Cave or not, we know perfectly well that you're still going to be spending a majority of your time at the office. Yes, the office, where sterile atmospheres help foster hate. Hiring a high-end chic designer to create a showplace entryway and a fancy playroom is one thing. We're talking about the spaces that often get ignored and matter more in the day-to-day operations.

There's not a lot you can do about the chicken-coop rows of cubes and cookie-cutter offices, all painfully illuminated by fluorescent lighting recently banned by the Geneva conventions.

But there are places where your Soloist sensibilities can tear through this despair. The dead zones: barren bathrooms. Long blank hallways. Featureless common areas. Lacking personality or spark, these "between" areas incubate hate like damp corners breed mold. Since these spaces are essentially abandoned, they tend to collect piles of random trash or just suffer from general neglect. They bring us down. Fight the darkness with light and ideas. Pop a media rack into an unused corner or along an empty wall. How about some art on the walls? Of a bathroom? Go on: break some rules – restaurants do it all the time. This is about more than the physical. In the few minutes when you literally let go, your mind is stimulated into new and unusual directions.

Take a cue from sports bars, world leaders in engaging their patrons during their frequent visits to "the facilities." Often one will find sections of the day's newspaper posted directly over the urinals. At the legendary Masters golf tournament in Augusta, Georgia, the premier clubhouse features TVs so the patrons don't miss a single putt.

For the retro part of your corporate bathroom, we recommend hanging pages from the *Wall Street Journal,* the *New York Times,* and the *Economist.* We also think it's stimulating to strategically place cool book titles and arresting magazine pages. Anything to distract you from the monotony of office chatter. Screens can show news, weather, sports updates, or even a voice-controlled interface so people can surf the Web hands free (a wise idea in the bathroom).

Hallways and walls are another dead zone. They frequently look deserted or, even worse, turn into overflow storage areas. You know, that corporate hillbilly look: dozens of filing boxes at crazy angles, garbage cans, rolled-up posters, reams of paper. Why? Again, there's no personal ownership. Okay, we can hear the facilities coordinators and office managers fretting that all that employee freedom will violate the Official Design Policy. But a reasonable amount of freedom can be invigorating. We know a film studio where staffers have free rein in decorating their offices and hallways – as long as the artwork is film related: movie posters, lobby cards, memorabilia, et cetera. When the decorations are someone's choice, they tend to be more thought provoking and fun.

Not surprisingly, IDEO wastes no walls or corners in its search to turn the workplace into an arena that celebrates both individual achievements and company innovations. You may have seen some of the colorful photos of the flagship offices near Stanford. (While coauthoring two books on the firm, Jonathan Littman had the good fortune to visit and work in IDEO offices on two continents.) The individual offices and cubes are pretty wild, but what's truly impressive are the broader touches – the stuff above: a full-size jib and snowboards with boots floating over partitions; sparkling bicycles suspended right over desks; and the Wing, a full-size replica of an airplane wing that hangs over a nifty project space. Murals and eclectic project displays enliven building entrances and team areas, featuring hot products and explorations of exotic materials, or even just hobbies. In San Francisco, a long wall is entirely taken up with a collection of packages – everything from Japanese soda cans to unusual beauty products – that looks like something out of a design museum.

The best of these Caves take an individual idea and spread it to the team or the company. For instance, the head of IDEO's Boston office knew something about acoustics and decided to have some gray soft-foam cubes made to hang like a cloud over his desk and soak up the noise. Being a designer, he arrayed the cubes in a structure similar to IDEO's four-squares logo. Staffers loved the cubes, and the office head bought three hundred more with the corporate goal of creating more logos throughout the office. But the cubes took on a life of their own. Soon their numbers had grown to nearly a thousand. Staffers grabbed every cube they could get their hands on and molded them into chairs and makeshift tables. We note something that IDEO wouldn't dare say: one reason the cubes caught on like wildfire was that they were excellent dividers, or, as we like to say, People-Keeper-Outers. Plus they became the weapon of choice for afternoon cube fights.

What the casual observer can't know, however, is that the reason the best IDEO offices enjoy such a vibrant pulse is that these dead zones are continually refreshed by a mixture of team and spontaneous individual efforts. There's a competitive element. The offices with the Soloists most willing to make an extra effort are the ones that year after year continuously reinvent themselves.

Fortunately, IDEO isn't the only firm that has caught wind of this trend.

We even know some companies that follow the café or restaurant model: letting an artist display his paintings for a month or two. If you're a manager or supervisor, you can give Sheeple something to graze on by challenging staff or project groups to become their own curators.

In the good old days, corporate giants were viewed as patrons of the arts, funding the local opera and ballet, and, of course, commissioning ridiculously expensive abstract sculptures and paintings for their outsize lobbies and public spaces. We're more interested in firms like Wells Fargo, Deere & Company, and Meredith Corporation, recognized by David Rockefeller's Business Committee for the Arts for not only doling out serious cash for professional artists, but also for incorporating arts initiatives and workplace exhibits into their offices.

Even better, in the past several years, Rockefeller's BCA has pushed its art@work, a program that encourages staffers to bring their creations and display them in the workplace. In companies such as General Mills, Estée Lauder, and Pfizer, BCA promotes the program as a way of "enhancing morale and building team spirit." We think it probably does boost morale, but for an entirely different reason.

Encouraging Soloists not only to create art but to share it with coworkers.

But we don't see why you should wait for an official program, grant, or corporate approval. And if you don't consider yourself particularly artistic, don't let that stop you.

Try hijacking products originally designed for homeowners. Chalkboard paint creates an erasable surface. Even better for businesses is a line of paint that transforms any section of wall into a dry-erase whiteboard with the stroke of a brush. And magnetic paint creates a wall that you can hang all sorts of things on.

The Green Cave

Increased telecommuting would save America 1.35 billion gallons of gas a year and stop twenty-six billion pounds of carbon dioxide from spewing into the atmosphere.

— Environmental Protection Agency

THE STARTER CAVE

Sometimes the easiest way to get started on office Cave dwelling is to begin in a safe, noncorporate locale. It's a way to experiment with the concept before you're comfortable going live in front of coworkers and management. Your Starter Cave may be little more than a cluttered garage or basement, an extra room, or even a large closet. Or something more official.

We're intrigued by a new phenomenon that we call the Cave Share. A few years after igniting in San Francisco, coworking facilities are spreading across the nation and around the globe. Coworking spaces offer Cave seekers a cross between the informality of a café and the business infrastructure and social stimulus of an office. Enthusiasts say the new work model offers a more open environment for sharing resources and exchanging ideas. Impromptu "free" brainstorms are common. Another big plus: with American Management Association reporting that nearly half of all companies snoop on their employees' Web surfing and e-mailing, there's something to be said for a Cave with a wiretap-free guarantee.

Coworking also offers flexibility. For instance, Independents Hall in Philadelphia offers such basics as broadband, desks, and access to a fully equipped conference room. Coworkers can buy full-time membership for $275 a month. So far, most coworkers have been independents and freelancers. But the Institute for the Future calls it a trend to watch over the next decade. We see a booming opportunity for mobile corporate warriors and their more forward-looking employers. Imagine the company cost savings if a staffer could pay just $3,000 a year for a fully equipped office – or a fraction of that for an occasional oasis. In New York, Sunshine Suites has been rolling out what reviewers call the "W Hotel" version, featuring slick private suites, locks, access to a rooftop perfect for company bashes, a Vermont retreat ideal for creative off-sites, and, yes, background checks to keep out freaks and corporate snoops.

DOWNCAVING

Karl Ronn of P&G, whom we met earlier, certainly earned the right to a traditional office. As the vice president of New Business at Procter & Gamble Health Care, he oversees a staff of six hundred and once had the traditional walls, ample square footage, and door. But a few years ago, he decided to put himself in a cube, surrounded by fifty other staffers. Ronn's reasons ranged from supporting innovation and increasing productivity to saving his own time. He says that being out in the company stream makes it easier for his staff when they "need twelve seconds" to ask a question or get feedback on a quick and dirty prototype. Those numerous minimeetings reduce obstacles faster, keep projects moving, and help avoid the biggest inefficiency. "By making myself available, I reduce the meetings that chew up hours – say, a [sensitive] personnel discussion that should have taken place five years ago."

Ronn laughs that the next thing he's got to do is shrink his cube. "I don't like the big cube. I'm not here most of the time. I don't need all that space. All it does is suggest that I must be important."

There are limits to how you can mold space at big corporations, but there are opportunities between the seams. One of Ronn's top staffers, Sofie Snauwaert, associate director of Baby Care Product Development, took the initiative in her group's community space. Like most corporations, P&G has conference rooms with massive tables that are less than inviting. That's when Snauwaert and staff came up with the idea to "get rid of the conference tables." She chucked the massive twenty-person tables and replaced them with comfortable couches. Wanting to give her teams a reason to come together, Snauwaert arranged for the purchase of Bodum coffeemakers.

"The tables made everything very formal. You do not get around these big conference tables and chat," says Snauwaert. She's dubbed the converted spaces team rooms.

Interestingly, they are not the place to do what's considered traditional work. "This is the place you hang out, and when you hang out together, good things happen."

Wherever you dig your first Cave, the key is to focus less on the stuff and more on the process.

Lots of budding Soloists start out with the highest hopes, and get a little carried away. A professor of business management we know says that the first thing he does is buy all the latest gear: copy machine, combination scanner/fax/printer, computer, phones, paper clips, file folders, file cabinets. Next he goes furniture crazy: $2,000 desk, $1,200 ergonomically correct chair, full-spectrum lighting. Recounting his story, he threw up his hands, reflecting on his mistakes. "I'd dig myself such a big hole by overspending on all this stuff that I felt under the gun. Now I had to produce."

You are the soul of your Cave, but where do you find its heart? High tech, low tech, no tech. Tropical, Zen, European. You need company? Add a fish, a bird, or a tarantula in a terrarium. What better place to put your spin cycle to watch the Bloomberg report at 7:00 a.m.? Or check your e-mail? We know someone who retrofitted a Lifecycle into his desk so he could pedal for hours while toiling at the computer. (He got very skinny.)

Caves demand gravitational pull. Create a mood and atmosphere. Paint is cheap. The basics go a long way: a great espresso machine, a sink, a well-stocked bar, and some tasty snacks in a minifridge. All these things will keep you from wandering off and losing track of what you were doing.

This brings us back to the central attraction of the Cave: it's your #1 hang. As with a kid's tree house, no one crashes your Cave without an invite. The Cave reflects more of you than any other physical place in your life – your office at work, your home, your bedroom. It's the perfect place to explore hobbies and new business interests that captivate you.

In the corporate setting, the *you* is mostly sanitized out of the equation. The Cave is where there is no contradiction in letting a hobby live next to a business pursuit. Where you embrace what most companies consider the colliding of worlds.

In your Cave, it's all you. And that's important.

Going on a buying splurge for the latest crap will not make you more productive. We have this naive belief that we need Things to ensure productivity – or, even worse, creativity.

Don't misunderstand. We aren't fans of minimalism. The other extreme can be equally problematic. Part of today's great technological illusion is that all you need to create a working office is a desk, a chair, a PC, and Microsoft Office. Software and furniture do not by themselves a great Cave make.

There's a lot to learn about Cave dwelling from Google, Pixar, Apple, and the like. These and other boxless companies are running with the idea that it's productive to create the corporate equivalent of a town square with great food, recreation, and cool places to hang.

We made some field trips to Google and Pixar to get a firsthand look at what makes these corporate Shangri-las. It's a no-brainer why these companies have become so successful and attractive to creative types. Their headquarters boast distinctive architecture and interiors that instantly set them apart from skyscrapers and office parks. At the Googleplex, Google's Mountain View headquarters, "Googlers" zip between buildings and meetings on bikes and motorized scooters. Security and custodial personnel roam the twenty-two-plus acres in little electric carts. T-shirts and cutoffs are typical for most of the year, creating the vibrant feel of a college campus. On the day we visited for a briefing on a branding project, the exotic sounds of a live Jamaican steel-drum band filled a central plaza. Entertainment is brought in throughout the year, enhancing a "lunch hour" that defies traditional meal and time constraints. There are sixteen restaurants on campus, with food and beverages provided free to all Googlers from dawn past dusk.

Interior office spaces are varied and unique. In one building, a couple of Googlers smack balls around a pool table, while nearby, someone busily prepares a presentation in a curtained alcove that houses a projector, a screen, and a score of comfortable chairs. Through glass walls, another half-dozen office spaces are visible. Discreet signs ask that pool players not "bang their cues on the floor," out of respect for people working nearby. Glass walls in more traditional office environments tend to produce a fishbowl effect: everyone's peering in, watching to see if you're getting your work done. At Google, the glass keeps everyone working in an open space, with the walls and doors helping to dampen the noise level.

Across the San Francisco Bay, in Emeryville, Disney's Pixar should feel like a movie studio. After all, Pixar has been cranking out major feature films since 1995's *Toy Story*. But since its films are produced by digital animation, the firm has server farms instead of soundstages and programmers instead of lights, cameras, and makeup. Pixar looks more like, well, Google than it does the back lot at Universal Studios. Again, sweeping architecture and a sense of space make this resemble some future Fantasyland. Unlike the multitude of buildings that make up the Googleplex, Pixar has one large main building and just a few outer structures.

During our several visits, scooter-riding "Pixies" shoot through the open central atrium, where ramps instead of stairs often lead off to hallways and offices. The atrium houses the nonstop refreshment zone: no need to step off to Starbucks when a Pixar barista is poised to quadruple-shot your latte for free. Meals at the Café Luxe, the upscale cafeteria, are served up from a menu that's changed daily by manager Luigi Passalacqua.

Pixies are encouraged to express themselves in decorating their spaces. Toys abound. An electric guitar. A lava lamp. A purple armchair. At other companies, corporate dictates against personalizing personal space often promote the fear that such decorating free fall might generate the downscale look of a nonprofessional flea market or funky bazaar. At Pixar, just as in the brightly colored, high-energy movies the company churns out, it all works.

We're excited about how companies like Google and Pixar are changing how corporations look at employees. They respect employee sensibilities and cater to their whims, while at the same time give them plenty of ways to play on the job. One ever-expanding caveat: employees who become too enamored of these company-sponsored distractions are in danger of spending even more time on the job than they would at a typical corporate setting. There's a phenomenon joked about called the Google 20 (as opposed to the Google 20 percent time); it's akin to the Freshman 15 at college campuses. It's a reference to the amount of weight one typically puts on during the first year on the job.

FAMOUS CAVES

The Fortress of Solitude

Fifty years ago, one of the world's most famous Caves made its dramatic first appearance. In Action Comics #241, the *Fortress of Solitude* made its big debut as the Cave away from the office for none other than Superman. Dug into a mountain in the wastes of the frozen north, the Fortress was occasionally featured as the hideaway that DC Comics' Man of Steel used when he needed a break from saving the world and dealing with his irritating coworkers at the *Daily Planet.*

Just as any Soloist might put up favorite mementos in his Cave, Superman had trophies from his past exploits, such as gigantic extraterrestrial creatures in his Interplanetary Zoo. Strangely, he was also a bit of a kiss ass: he had an entire room in his Fortress dedicated to his boss, Perry White.

The important takeaway: Superman is only really able to get away when he visits the arctic Fortress. Because his annoying "pal" Jimmy Olsen — the consummate Minute Man — can't fly, he can't bug him at the Fortress. And in between outwitting arch nemesis Lex "Bulldozer" Luthor and clobbering the interdimensional Switchblade Mr. Mxyzptlk, Superman finds plenty of time to Solocraft in his arctic hideout. There isn't even any cell service, which means Yackety Yak girlfriend Lois Lane can only leave voice mail. Whether Superman is puttering around in his laboratory, tuning up his army of Superman robots, or just burning stuff in his atomic disintegrator pit, this should serve as a lesson to us all that even a comic-book character needs to get away every once in a while.

Where is *your* Fortress of Solitude?

Bulging waistlines aside, true Soloists at these companies can really shine. They're given a green light to chase down side projects of interest. Whether you're lucky enough to work at one of today's Soloist-friendly companies or not, digging your Cave is about taking these concepts to an individual level. Make your Cave a campus of one. That way, you never have to leave.

SQUARE ONE

If you're shaking your head, thinking Cave dwelling is not for you, think again. There's a Cave on every corner ... and you've probably been there today.

We are the Starbucks generation. Old, young, and everything in between, we think nothing of spending part of our workday in a coffee joint. The attractions are multiple.

1. It's not the coffee in your office.
2. It's not the people in your office.
3. It's not the office.

Starbucks has been a beautiful invention for corporate America, a perfect fit for what used to be called the Kinko's phenomenon: the twenty-five to thirty million Americans who log serious hours outside a traditional office. Even our crusty federal government is pushing for up to a quarter of its workforce to at least occasionally telework. For those confined to cubes – about 70 percent of those in corporate jobs – coffee joints are as close as many get during most workdays to a minivacation.

The international chain has given millions of American

workers a ready excuse to play hooky for thirty minutes at a shot. And if you're worried about your boss busting your chops, just bring him back a double-shot nonfat caramel mochaccino. Designer coffee has legitimized office performance enhancement. Break-room coffee is to café brew what vitamins are to steroids.

This ritual is embraced as a sign of a dedicated staffer. If you're getting juiced, you're obviously going to get so much more work done when you finally bounce your wired ass back to the office. There are never any questions asked when you pull a coffee run. Twenty minutes. Half an hour. Longer. People are more than willing to indulge you when you're bringing them back a fix.

That time alone at the coffeehouse begins to take on a hallowed quality. You're breaking free of the cage. It's not quite your living room, but it's not far off. There are armchairs, sofas, even fireplaces. People who don't look like your fellow office drones.

Soloists are grabbing a cuppa for an hour or two to get clear of the office people they hate in order to focus and concentrate on a project. Why? The people you're likely to encounter in a café – unlike in your company – are reasonably well behaved. Most tend to come and go. Starbucks says 70 percent leave within five minutes. Those who stick around tend to be glued to their screens.

USA TODAY recently documented evidence of the Soloist trend. At a hip San Francisco café, it noted that up to twenty teleworkers at a time regularly frequent the bohemian joint for what one thirty-five-year-old called "the good lighting, the right chair, and the vibe of the people."

Finding the perfect café is a highly personal matter. Tom Zimmerman at IBM has discovered that, like many

The Time Cave

What if your day is so overloaded and your company so tightly buttoned down that you can't imagine creating a Cave? Consider the Time Cave. Like most busy corporate professionals, Sofie Snauwaert finds it tough to grab thirty to sixty minutes a day without a whirlwind of intrusions. Her solution? She rises at 5:00 a.m., before, as she puts it, "the house comes to life." Sometimes she'll read, but more often she will sit in front of a blank piece of paper, "jotting down my thoughts and doodles." Snauwaert loves fine pens and stationery and enjoys the feel of them in her hand.

The Time Cave is beyond space or place. If your company won't permit a Cave and a custom Cave is beyond your budget, consider carving one out of a part of your day. It's the dedicated time and solitude that matters. A moment out of your day to nourish the Soloist within.

corporate people today, he often has to get out of the office. "When I've got a lot of writing to do – papers, proposals, patents – I go to a café to be alone and concentrate," he says. His favorite is the Coffee Society across from De Anza College in Cupertino. "It's filled with students, and what students provide is this energy of work," he says. Most have books and laptops, and Zimmerman finds the mood and pulse a welcome break from his routine. "You go to the office and that's just working, not much joy, the furrowed brow." Zimmerman hits his Cave about nine, works until noon, lunches, and then if he's lucky returns for another hour or two. He rarely takes cell calls at the coffee shop and used to never go online.

Café Cave dwellers rhapsodize about the buzz of the plugged-in crowd. They feel bolstered by fellow surrogate coworkers (who we note never ask, "Where the hell is that report?"). Experts tell us this phenomenon largely derives from Pavlovian impulses, deeply embedded from years of office or university conditioning, from the need to be encircled by busyness to be busy ourselves. Action, activity, the atmosphere of work. It's a bit like people who benefit by going to the gym, surrounded by people pumping iron, running on the treadmill, doing sit-ups. You don't nap in a café, and you generally don't goof off. The modern café code discourages the very interruptions, small talk, and chitchat that make office life so repellent. Perhaps it's because everybody's transfixed by their laptops or talking on their cells, working and making sales calls. The café is the church of the modern mobile worker. Interrupt or otherwise annoy your fellow café Cave dwellers, and you risk decavement.

There's little tolerance for people who don't abide by the unwritten code. To effectively use these places as your mobile Cave, there are a few customs to be observed.

- ► Order.
- ► Spend.
- ► Tip.

Just as you don't cross the office manager, treat your baristas with respect. Make sure they notice you stuffing that buck in that tip jar once or twice a week.

You'll get a thank-you or at the very least a smile. The real benefit is that they'll soon know your order and you'll no longer have to talk to them. One less person to hate.

What happens if you don't tip? The Barista's Revenge. We know at least one barista who tracks cheapskates. And messes with them by randomly switching out their regular rocket fuel for decaf.

Today, on-the-go Cave dwellers have a range of outlets. New slants on the café, bakery, and small restaurants designed to quench our growing desire to drink, eat, and work at some place that is neither the home nor the office. Consider the rise of Panera Bread, which has quickly expanded to more than twelve hundred locations, by combining Starbucks-style Wi-Fi and comfortable seating with Mediterranean-style food.

Ron Shaich, the company's CEO, has been actively selling the business press about the getaway appeal his bistros offer to corporate refugees looking for a break from stale office surroundings. "We now live in a society where cubicles are considered the corporate equivalent of a tenement," says Shaich. "What's most efficient for business and employee alike is a measure of flexibility."

YOUR CAR AS CAVE

The American love affair with the car is alive and well. The machine has become so ingrained in our lives that it's become a part of us. A four-thousand-pound careening metal part of us. Sometimes we're so busy behind the wheel that we forget we're driving. We're talking on the phone. Eating. Drinking. Putting on makeup. Shaving. Watching movies. Texting. Everything but focusing on keeping the car on the road. So it may seem odd that we'd advocate Solocrafting on top of all your other extracurricular driving duties.

But it works.

According to literary legend, Vladimir Nabokov, the celebrated author of *Lolita,* enjoyed writing in his car with a pencil and index cards (and hopefully one hand on the wheel). These days, it's not a strange sight to see workers on the go parked outside cafés and restaurants, accessing their Wi-Fi services to take care of online duties.

The secret is to make Solocrafting on wheels effortless without adding to the distractions. A lot of people use this time – during the commute or on a long drive to visit a client – to return voice mails or even e-mails. E-mails?! Yes, take a look. Some of those jokers in the cars around you are using their smartphones in a dumb way: to type and send e-mails.

In some states you may even be breaking the law.

Hang up and log out already! This is your chance for blessed isolation.

THE PLAYHOUSE

One of the first Cave types to receive national attention is what we call the Playhouse, a trend driven by refugees. Men uprooted from their own homes. Unable to call any room their own, they're creating spaces where their hobbies and interests can thrive without the poison of family interference. The Playhouse recalls a childhood-era fort or tree house. Invariably, someone is to be excluded: kids, wives, husbands, boyfriends, girlfriends, pets, and interloping neighbors.

James B. Twitchell, a professor at the University of Florida, recently published *Where Men Hide,* celebrating in words and pictures what he calls hidey-holes, men turning garages, attics, and backyard sheds into places to get away and work or pursue other interests. His book notes in great detail that there are ample positive reasons for men to continue to seek out an Other Place, not the least of them being the disappearance of men's athletic clubs, fraternal orders, university clubs, and barbershops. We agree. We view the hidey-hole as a source of pride. And we'd like to invite the better half to join the phenomenon. Women, too, are digging out their own Caves.

Today, the Home Cave can be everything from a place to pursue a budding hobby to an incubator for a new startup or business venture. Size isn't everything. Dave Monks, a fortysomething lawyer in San Francisco, decided he needed a place to unwind in his partner's apartment. His hidey-hole was a five-by-six-foot closet. "It's literally a cave," he told the *New York Times*. "I moved in a desk, my computer and my movie memorabilia, and I can be in there for hours at a time."

There are clear advantages to the Home Cave: no travel time. No time clock. And if you don't have a great view, there are always posters, paintings, and photos of your choice, without any fear that you're violating "corporate protocol."

THE ROAMING CAVE

Sometimes the Home Cave is not quite home. Dave Elchoness, an entrepreneur in the virtual-worlds arena, has turned his Colorado backyard into a Cave – his place to think and be alone and explore ideas. "I have a wife, two children, two cats, two dogs," he told us. "Needless to say, the house is freakin' bedlam. The weather here is awesome, so I can do this most of the year. I have the trees and the grass and the peace and quiet." Elchoness also enjoys cigars, so now he's got a Cave where he can smoke his stogies and think in the shadows of the Rockies.

But while the home and backyard aren't bad Starter Caves, the only limit is your imagination. For many people, their Cave is a favorite park bench or in the shade of a giant oak tree. Nor must your Cave be a cage. Many people love a glade or a walking trail. A Cave can crisscross with a place one might journey while Island Hopping, a temporary getaway strategy we'll talk about in the following chapter.

Sometimes following the path will lead you to the Cave. "I needed to do something – anything – to move myself out of this stuck place," Paul Smith, an environmental consultant, told us. "So I pointed my car towards the East Bay hills." He began to see signs for outdoor theaters and parks, then a little sign for Sequoia Arena. He found an amazing collection of plants, flowers, and animals, and a pyramid, all dedicated to poet Joaquin Miller.

Sequoia Arena has since become the place where Smith goes to clear his mind and find inspiration. Struggling one day with an application essay for an MBA program, he walked down Big Trees Trail and found himself drawn to a perch just above the pulsing city life of Oakland. He happened to have his laptop along and knew where to go: just off the well-beaten path, there is a circle of the remains of trees. He sat down, took out his laptop, and began an inspirational essay that got him into Presidio School of Management. He went on to open his own environmental consulting firm, GreenSmith Consulting. And yes, he still makes regular pilgrimages to the outdoor amphitheater known as Sequoia Arena.

The Roaming Cave has broad appeal. "I'll take my laptop and go somewhere only as long as it holds its charge," says Shane Elliott, the interactive advertising developer. He finds it relaxing to go to the Grove — a popular outdoor mall near L.A.'s Farmers Market — and sit on a bench and work. Or he'll head out to a park and work on a blanket. And he considers it striking gold when his wanderings bring him in range of a random Wi-Fi signal.

Entire companies are going stark raving nomad. The *Economist* recently documented the trend in "Labour Movement," featuring the tale of how Pip Coburn started an investment consultancy with a handful of employees in 2005. The first company meeting was in a Manhattan coffee shop, and the first order of business was to order a fleet of BlackBerrys. Eight months in, with seven employees, Coburn Ventures had all the trappings of a modern-day financial firm. Except one. "No client ever even asked me whether we had an office," Coburn told the *Economist*. To date, he's yet to have a compelling reason to bother with a brick-and-mortar locale. Everyone's being way too productive and having far too much freedom.

Back when Coburn was drudging at the global bank UBS, he had to drop out of bed at 5:00 a.m. to catch the commuter train to Manhattan to make it to his cube by 6:45. Now he awakens more than an hour later, and has time to exercise before flipping on his BlackBerry at 6:45 a.m. His office: the Wi-Fi cafés of Westchester, or his home. That independence also led Coburn to write a well-received business book about why some technologies succeed, *The Change Function*.

But turning the world into a Cave for the upstart company generated growing pains. At first, there were somewhat impersonal interactions among employees, Coburn told the *Economist,* and a lack of what he called "casual serendipity." With no watercooler to gabble around, there's little chance for making synchronistic connections. Coburn solved that problem by creating regular friendly get-togethers.

By not making these gatherings mandatory, the Ensemble built stronger, real-world connections. The phenomenon of wandering workers has become prevalent enough that an academic study has been done. Gloria Mark and Norman Makoto Su, both in the Department of Informatics at UC Irvine, recently completed their "Designing for Nomadic Work" report, an exploration of an "extreme form of mobile work," to better understand the practices of the professionals who toil out of the office extensively. Their conclusion: nomadic workers employ similar behavior strategies to wandering peoples through the ages, including pastoral nomads, Micronesian navigators, and tribal chiefs. Factors in common include using "principal actants" for survival (the means to accomplish their work – namely, the components for their portable office), seeking resources (power for their computer, cell-phone reception, a space with a desk or table), and integrating with others (coworkers both nomadic and non-nomadic).

We applaud tools, methods, or devices that expand your ability to mark off your territory and express yourself. A key Soloist retreat, the Cave is a huge part of who you are, and who you might become. It's all part of the transformation from corporate gray to a place beyond hate where you know you can get some work done.

Here's to your Cave. Happy digging.

12. Island Hopping

"How often I found where I should be going only by setting out for somewhere else."

— R. BUCKMINSTER FULLER

We did a lot of poking around to discover how people describe their typical day. Guess what? People are either painfully dull or they flip on the lying switch when asked how they spent their workday.

Believe it or not, millions of American workers break their days into ten-minute increments. They're eager to report exactly what they do to journalists and websites focusing on the workplace. Yet U.S. workers almost never fess up to anything but the predictable routine.

The typical American corporate day (according to the workers) runs pretty much like this:

Check and return e-mail and voice mail.
Hope and pray the work's getting done.
Meetings.
Sit at desk and eat the thing brought back for you.
More meetings.
Hope and pray the work's getting done.
Check and return e-mail and voice mail.
Rinse and repeat.

What's missing is outside stimulus. Lots of people barely leave their desk, let alone the building. Consider the biological functions. They offer sad details of meals: "Food from the deli comes in" or "Lunch at my desk – again" or "Eating at my desk while working." Some even confess they are kept so busy they have to do the "pee-pee dance" because bathroom breaks are frowned upon. Don't believe it? We found some firms that might fairly be described as bordering on the anal compulsive. They attempt to "roster" bathroom breaks in an effort to increase productivity. Supervisor approval is required if you've got to "go" outside of scheduled times – no matter how urgent the call of nature. Consider the claimed absence of play. Studies show that most corporate folks surf the Internet to catch up on sports teams and celebrities, play video games, and e-mail friends. It's how you stay in the mix today. But when people talk publicly about their workday, they hide these Soloist tendencies, loath to admit a personal life or any pursuit that doesn't directly generate profit.

We found successful executives who had no fear of confessing they regularly use games in the office to stay focused throughout the day – right at their desk. Men like startup executive Steve Viarengo, who says, "It may sound counterintuitive, but I often pop up a game of hearts or solitaire on my computer." Viarengo says it lets his mind reset and clears his head. He only plays for two to three minutes at a time, but he says it makes him better able to approach his next challenge. "It's like eating that little bit of ginger before eating the next piece of sushi. It's my refresh."

Sadly, Viarengo is the exception. Few people confess to leaving the building for anything but officially sanctioned meetings. If they do take lunch, it must be with a client or partner, aka the "power lunch." We read dozens of these "day in the life"s on the Web, and only three or four individuals fessed up to a coffee break or any other break, in spite of overwhelming evidence to the contrary. E-mail and phone calls are their main contact with the outside world. Very few admit to spending even a couple of minutes reading anything outside of the stuff directly applicable to their work.

There is a hamster-wheel futility to the work lives described by these professional unfortunates. Here's how one branding executive says he began one day from 9:00 to 10:00 a.m.: "Meet with market-research department to discuss specifics of your latest round of quantitative research. You are trying to understand why people are not repurchasing your product, but you don't feel that the data presented actually answers your questions. You decide that you'll need to design another round of research – but where's the money going to come from?"

Instead of considering product improvements or visiting stores or customers to find out why his product stinks, this branding suit blindly trudges on the corporate Tread-mill to Nowhere, asking people who don't care or can't be bothered to keep pumping out mindless data.

Compare this to how a fashion designer starts her day, as described to the career website Vault.com.

"9:00 to 12:00: Climb out of bed and go shopping. (In this position, you actually go shopping to see what's out on the market. You watch the trends. Then, you try to incorporate what you see – new colors, fabrics, trends – into your designs.)" This enterprising woman then got on the phone and talked to "trend experts," flipped through dozens of magazines while eating lunch, and, in general, exposed herself to as many ideas and influences as possible every hour of her day. A technique called Design Thinking.

Outside perspectives are critical to all kinds of businesses. Getting outside can be a state of mind. There are places right within your halls and cubicles where you can get the peace of mind you need. Cave Digging, as we just learned, is all about finding and creating cool, useful places to do doses of work. Here we're exploring Island Hopping: strategies devoted to getting away from work, both physically and mentally. Breaking free to focus on something different for a while or just a change of scenery – either of which can help recharge a Soloist's batteries.

One of the most promising experiments to date began with a pair of guerrilla fighters at the unlikely Minnesota headquarters of Best Buy, the national electronics chain. When a couple of managers realized their teams were floundering, some HR people with a soft spot for Soloists offered a bold experiment. They called it a results-only work environment – ROWE. "There would be no mandatory meetings," wrote *BusinessWeek* of the plan. "No times when you had to physically be at work. Performance would be based on output, not hours."

Neither the HR gurus nor the managers told the higher-ups. The movement spread virally. The workers branded their laptops with ROWE stickers – but most of all, they vanished. One employee began spending healthy chunks of his workweek with his Remington 12 gauge – hunting, or off in a boat, fishing. Another took long afternoon bike rides. The loose reins didn't result in the "Gone Fishing" folks abandoning their responsibilities. Hourly workers still got in their time, albeit sometimes after night had fallen. Productivity increased. The Gone Fishing people outperformed the downbutt office people. The ROWE renegades took their findings to Best Buy's CEO, who agreed to extend the new strategy to other divisions. It's hard to know how far this burgeoning movement will go. Best Buy claims ROWE teams have shown an average productivity increase of 41 percent. The two Soloists who concocted the scheme, Cali Ressler and Jody Thompson, wrote a book, *Why Work Sucks and How to Fix It,* and have spun off a consulting arm called CultureRx to spread its thinking to *Fortune* 500 companies.

If the Spreadsheets and Stop Signs would get out of the way, this is how most offices would function. A realization that it's what you do – not where you do it – that matters. As that Best Buy guy who liked to fire off his shotgun during the workweek told *BusinessWeek,* "It used to be that I had to schedule my life around my work. Now, I schedule my work around my life."

It would rock if this were the Soloist spirit supported by most companies.

It's not.

> *"I hate that guy in my office who is a smoker and takes about 15 breaks a day to go outside and smoke. As a non-smoker, I do not get the same amount of time to 'do nothing' every day. I even tried to take a 'non-smoking' break several times, but that didn't go over too well . . ."*
>
> — FROM THE PUBLIC FORUM ON PEERTRAINER.COM

People will hate you for having the audacity to get out of the office. Yeah, that's right: hate. The office-bound at Best Buy, for instance, resented the office-free. They did everything possible to malign and strangle the project.

The important takeaway here is that it's possible to change the status quo. Just like Best Buy's ROWE team, you may have to start out flying under the radar. With luck – and an enlightened member of management or two – your proof of concept may one day become lauded and supported by the Powers That Be.

FIND YOUR ISLANDS

> *A sly rabbit will have three openings to its den.*
>
> — CHINESE PROVERB

Island Hopping generates the same psychic relaxation and escape that we feel on a weekend getaway in Jamaica: beach, palm trees, blue drinks, bikinis, turquoise waters, and no e-mail. There are islands all around us but we're not trained to see them, or willing to take the few minutes required to enjoy the separation they provide from our "real world." Island Hopping is a chance to unplug and let your batteries recharge. Permission to slip off the work grid for a while, and vanish from the radar of your coworkers, boss, and staff.

The traditional model of Island Hopping includes taking off Friday afternoon to play golf with partners or clients, going to the ball game, or maybe taking in the ponies at the track. We believe in broadening the range of islands you visit. Imagine having a whole ballpark as your personal Island. The marketing director for a major sports facility deals with fifty full-time employees milling around all the time, which swells to more than two hundred people on event days. The same keys that lock the door to what her coworkers call her Dungeon – a converted utility room that she chose as her office – also grant her access to the sixty-thousand-seat sports stadium. It's her sunny-day getaway just steps from the Dungeon. "I go sit alone in the stands and read a book while getting some sun."

Libraries make for excellent Islands since yapping tends to get shushed. Art museums and galleries are even quieter, and obviously feature abundant creative inspiration. Parks offer fresh air and nature in controlled environments. Beaches have unique personalities, and restaurants are ideal, as long as you don't overstay your welcome. Gyms have become the Soloist's new multipurpose self-improvement center – the place many busy managers and executives do their reading while simultaneously burning off carbs spinning or even treadmilling. Some even use the pause between weight-lifting reps to read reports. Then there are trains, buses, and ferries. Besides saving you from having to hate other drivers, leaving the piloting to others gives you license to work – without having to answer the phone or e-mail.

Islands aren't always about place. Sometimes they're about passion. Maybe it's a hobby you can even do at your desk. Crossword puzzles, sudoku, scrapbooking. Diversions that become almost meditative, freeing you for a bit from the drone of work projects.

THE BIG ISLAND

If you're open to it, you'll come to find that passion or hobby that becomes your Big Island: a place broad and varied enough to explore and return to for inspiration and relaxation again and again. To some, these might be intellectual pursuits. For example, many executives and managers are fascinated by history and become experts in specific periods – say, the American Revolution – reading widely, visiting museums and monuments, and steeping themselves in the wisdom and challenges of another age. This passion reflects their character and becomes something novel they bring to their careers, sometimes even applying their knowledge to how they manage and explore new ideas. Just as important, it often becomes a bridge to other talented men and women in business. Many take up playing an instrument as adults and get tremendous satisfaction out of performing with fellow enthusiasts. Art offers the dual joys of creation and collecting.

Technical advances have made it possible for amateurs to explore their pursuits farther than ever before. Anyone with a decent telescope and some knowledge of the heavens can see other worlds only astronomers could explore a century ago. The Internet and Google have opened up research troves once only attainable by professional researchers or trained librarians.

It is the depth of your pursuit that feeds your Soloist passions. Carl Haney, the P&G veteran, began getting serious about buying and studying wine – not to mention drinking it – more than fifteen years ago. While working in London in the early 1990s he and a friend began scoring some plum purchases at Christie's auctions. One day in 2000, in his office in Baltimore, Haney received a mysterious letter listing the name of a restaurant, the time to arrive, and the instruction "Bring two bottles of wine." There was no name or return address on the envelope.

Haney accepted the curious invitation, enjoying fine cuisine with several successful men, accompanied, of course, by a tasting of a few fine vintages, including two from his collection: a 1982 Chateau Leoville-Las Cases and a 1989 Chateau Cos d'Estournel. Not only were Haney's wines voted best of the dinner, but right there on the spot, he was inducted into the group, the Dogs of Wine. Over the next several years, Haney found the club a unique window into a talented, elite group – everyone from the CFO of a top financial firm to a key IRS lawyer, a banker, a premier radiologist, and a top writer for a national wine magazine. Membership rules were simple. Each of the Dogs was required to put on a dinner once a year at which he could invite two guests. If you couldn't attend a dinner, you could send a substitute. Best of all, once a year, the Dogs of Wine would toss one member the group had come to hate. Nothing personal. The club wanted fresh blood, yet wanted to keep the Ensemble to a manageable ten. The Dogs of Wine and Haney's continuing passion for the fruit of the vine have proved a tremendous asset to his career, affording him an extra level of confidence during the countless business lunches and dinners he attends every year. Eight years in, and he's yet to be voted off the island. The hobby has given him a critical bridge to starting and maintaining business relationships. "I can sit and taste wine and talk about it with any CEO," says Haney. "It's a huge equalizer."

> *"Ich bin reif für die Insel."*
> — FAMOUS GERMAN PHRASE. ENGLISH TRANSLATION: "I'M RIPE FOR THE
> ISLAND," THE EQUIVALENT OF "I NEED A VACATION."

SPONTANEOUS ISLAND HOPPING

Today, smart office humans are taking control of their fitness, realizing it plays a key role in their daily performance and that health and appearance matter in the corporate sphere. Island Hoppers work out at a lot of places besides the gym. We know Silicon Valley businesspeople who catch real waves before work, executives in Reno who take a few ski runs on weekday afternoons, and Wall Streeters who rock climb in Central Park. We don't all have easy access to the surf, slopes, or big boulders. But corporations are getting the clue that exercise doesn't have to be limited to before or after work.

Studies show just minutes of morning exercise jolts mental performance for several hours. In the afternoon, it can chase off that postlunch bogdown. People are striding up five flights of stairs to deliver a report instead of waiting for the crammed elevator – getting the bonus of a wonderful escape from a detested People Hating experience. Mayo Clinic recently concluded a real-world study of the effects of increased activity in the workplace. Endocrinologist James Levine's idea was that even a little movement throughout the day promotes weight loss as well as maintains good health and increases productivity. Levine set up a kind of "Office of the Future" for eighteen employees at the Minneapolis professional staffing firm SALO, outfitting the office with a walking track and treadmill desks ("walkstations"), replacing traditional phones with headsets, and adding a massage chair and active games like Wii Fit, a pool table, foosball, and basketball. Levine hoped to confirm his earlier work, in which he demonstrated that people who blend moderate, regular movement into their everyday routines are more likely to reach and maintain healthy body weight than are those doing "power work-outs" or even structured exercise. Though the study group was composed of office drones, they were also "very busy, active people who liked the idea of incorporating movement into their regular workplace activity," said Levine. "That's exactly what they did" during the experiment. The results were impressive.

The eighteen volunteers lost a total of 156 pounds during the six-month study – an average of 8.8 pounds each, 90 percent of which was body fat. The nine participants who had expressed an interest in losing weight as part of the research shed even more blubber: 15.4 pounds each. Cholesterol levels dropped an average of 37 percent.

Spreadsheets even found reason to cheer. Far from costing the company lost productivity, the new activity environment led the group to nail its highest-ever monthly revenue at the midpoint of the research. (Show *that* to your supervisor, and maybe you can score your department a pool table.)

But not all random Island Hopping has to happen at the office.

Shane Elliott, the online advertising-agency designer, lays down a couple of days of work from the Home Cave. Still, after a long stretch surrounded by your stuff, home can seem like a jumbo cubicle. So it helps to hop away. "I'll have a ten-hour day and give myself a bunch of different breaks," he says. "I'll take a long lunch or drive across town just to see a friend. Go see a movie in the middle of the day. Call someone to meet me for coffee. Hell, I'll even do laundry to have a change of pace."

For another kind of break, Elliott enjoys calculating his salary for, say, a three-hour chunk of work. "I add that up and then go and spend it on something. That feels pretty good!" This commercial destination turns out to be a very popular Island. "Retail Therapy" is what another eight-to-fiver called it. "I love cooking, so I'll take a break during the day and just wander around Williams-Sonoma, which is right down the street," Gregory told us. "I'm always finding new things for the kitchen. And I don't stop there: 'Let's see what I need at Neiman Marcus!' "

The more skilled you become at hopping to your Islands, the more productive and creative you are likely to become at your daily tasks. Just remember to exercise caution around the office Spreadsheets and Stop Signs. The punch-clock mentality is not dead.

"A long time ago I discovered that I was more productive, and that my work was of better quality, if I spent some time each day doing something completely unrelated to writing books. In years past this has, at different times, taken the form of doing construction work, boat-building, model rocketry, writing code, and playing around with electronic circuits."

— NEAL STEPHENSON, AUTHOR OF *SNOW CRASH*

ISLAND HOPPING AT YOUR DESK

Play is the new work.

A major provider of online games recently conducted a survey about casual gaming habits at work with more than five hundred people who compete on the company's website. Some of the surprising responses: more than 80 percent of respondents who play online games during the workday feel better focused on work as a result of these periodic mental breaks. Improved productivity was reported by 76 percent. Nearly three-quarters said that they rely on game breaks to reduce job-related stress.

People are clearly Island Hopping at work. The survey concludes that a third of respondents play online games during working hours. Just over half (52 percent) play occasionally throughout the day – and not during lunchtime or other "official" breaks. Hitting the e-games is a brief excursion. Game breaks seldom total more than thirty minutes of the day for most players. While your cube neighbors are vacantly staring at beige fabric walls and pushpinned agendas, consider the cube-with-a-view strategy. You don't need the Internet or a cell phone or any other technology to take a break. "I do virtual Island Hopping all day with pictures around my cube," says Samantha, a product-development staffer at an energy firm. "I've plastered my cube with all the places I've traveled, pictures of the outdoors and my friends and family." The many striking photos of France, America, and Belize give her several tiny Islands to journey to every day – even if each voyage only lasts seconds. "The photos give me a renewed sense of why I'm at my desk," she says. "I can travel and explore and fund those adventures."

Lisa Carmel, the veteran of British Petroleum and Procter & Gamble, takes what she calls community-service breaks. "You'd think you'd cue up all your community service for when you're not busy," she says. But if Carmel is going to be working a lot, she'll find herself thinking, "I'll finish this Excel spreadsheet, then I can spend ten to fifteen minutes making calls for the library foundation." Carmel finds these little Islands "incredibly fun and rewarding." She may not get paid, but she gets to "meet really interesting people," and it makes her feel good.

Personal do-gooding is catching on in corporations, and whether or not you feel the impulse, there's something smart and rewarding about doing good beyond your desk. Umpqua Bank, headquartered in Portland, Oregon, with 147 branches, has formalized community-service breaks. Employees get one week of paid time a year to volunteer for any local cause that inspires them. Ditto at MITRE, where many staffers spent their week supporting Hurricane Katrina relief efforts. And even in the 24/7 world of Silicon Valley, the idea is making inroads. At the computer firm Intuit, employees get four days of paid leave per year to do good.

Break time is increasingly being woven into the physical fabric of the workplace. Many companies are transforming areas within their offices with comfortable fun furniture, video-game consoles, TVs, and amenities that would have shocked business leaders just a decade ago. And not just electronic diversions. A favorite pastime at Sony-owned Crackle.com is the low-tech Ping-Pong table just off the lunchroom. Employees frequently slip off during the day to play in the perpetual pickup tournament. Even management likes to smack the ball around.

The importance of a workday break has long been recognized. The first official Island Hop traces its origins to the turn of the twentieth century. One account credits the Barcolo Manufacturing Company of Buffalo, which, in 1902, agreed to employee demands for a short break in the morning and afternoon – dubbed the coffee break.

Only recently has science proved the benefits of what every lunch-loopy worker already knew: it helps to take a rest during the workday. Ironically, by studying the rat race – literally, rats running in a maze – researchers at MIT and other institutions have discovered breaks help us learn new tasks. The scientists gave the rats the equivalent of a coffee break immediately after a race. The rats' brain waves showed patterns identical to those when they scurried through the maze, only in reverse, playing over and over, and at twenty times the speed of the original patterns. The scientists said this was an indication that the rats were internalizing the experience.

The takeaway for business rats: your coffee break may be invaluable. The trick may be in taking a break immediately after performing complex or creative work: rehearsing an upcoming presentation, brainstorming, analyzing a

Grab Some ZZZs

The research is in. Snoozing at your desk is good for business. Abundant studies by everyone from NASA to leading universities have proven a number of brain benefits — improvements in learning, memory, and cognition. Advantages of sleeping on the job can come from as brief as a few-minute micro-nap to a full twenty-minute power nap. Corporate cogs once feared the workday nap as a potentially fireable offense. But in the past few years, even more conservative firms like Procter & Gamble have installed cushy EnergyPods by MetroNaps, comfortable recliners that make it easy to catch a few winks even in a noisy workspace. But is allowing employees to nap on the company dime worth the investment? Our advice to managers: sleep on it.

key report. (Warning: Under no circumstances should you ever take a break immediately after a People Hating encounter. If you're forced to relive a run-in with the office Bulldozer over and over, your head might explode.)

Creative groups on deadline often thrive on the fast pace – and the breaks. "It seems like we're always running," says Kyle Johnston, the Web and digital creative director at Garmin International. "When a product comes out, all the other divisions get all the time they need, until it gets to us. Then we have a month or two before we pass it on to marketing." How do they get the work done fast? "We spend a lot of time taking little breaks. We have a gas station across the street to get drinks or snacks. There is a small group of people who are RC car enthusiasts. We bring in a Wii to play occasionally." And when Johnston's group

DO SOME DOODLING

Chances are you doodle. Faber-Castell (the pencil heads) surveyed a thousand adults to discover that 93 percent of people under the age of twenty-five doodle at various times throughout the day. The numbers tumble as people age — down to 60 percent by the time they hit sixty-five. Doodles are to art what scribbles are to writing: meaningless lines. Sure, they can take on shape and form — who hasn't been blown away by someone two chairs down at a conference, creating a masterpiece in his notebook? But the important thing to remember is that there is no Bureau of Doodle Standards ready to judge your chicken scratches. The doodle is like taking a walk without leaving your desk. An imagination quickie.

A lot of doodling in the office takes place when people are on the phone, and one executive we interviewed swears by it. "Doodling allows me to stay focused," she says. "If I'm spending time on a call, in order to stay focused, I doodle. That way my mind doesn't wander."

CEOs, executives, managers — even presidents of the United States doodle. Doodles have been preserved from administrations as far back as Thomas Jefferson's in 1801. One of Herbert Hoover's scribbles inspired a line of children's pajamas. Ronald Reagan was such a gifted doodler that he'd dash off cartoons to members of his staff.

Men prefer squares, rectangles, designs with straight lines, and cars. Women dig circles and curves, while a quarter of doodlers both male and female toss in symbols like stars and arrows, as well as the occasional body part — a hand, an eye — or sometimes a stick figure.

Even the most primitive images can assist you in visualizing elements of your job that aren't remotely artistic. Innovation experts believe doodling may help free your mind during a brainstorm — or just during ordinary thinking. Many argue you're better off doodling during a brainstorm — freeing your right brain — than taking notes. Expressing yourself visually in even the simplest way can help you come up with new ideas.

You might even profit from your doodles. In 1967, Texas entrepreneur Rollin King sketched a triangle on the back of a cocktail napkin. He labeled the corners Dallas, Houston, and San Antonio, to show his lawyer the basic route plan for a small competitive airline. Four years later, King and the lawyer, Herb Kelleher, kicked off Southwest Airlines.

But there's another great reason to doodle.

Consider doodling the nearest Island. When there's just minutes before that next meeting. Or not enough time for a nap. The doodle is an act of independence. Now it's your chance to sit at your desk and look busy as you studiously work up a doodle. Just let it flow. Let the pen skate across the paper — lines, swoops, curlicues — and before you know it, you're caught up in the Zen of the doodle. You've reached an Island in just a minute or two, an Island that just may help you get your work done or spark an inspiration.

To all those Sheeple who fear doodling might be a fireable offense, check this out: Sofie Snauwaert of P&G proudly showed her doodles to her twelve-year-old recently, only to have her daughter exclaim, "Mom, what if your boss sees that?"

Snauwaert replied with a chuckle, "I do them in front of my boss."

completes a big project, it takes a big break smack in the middle of the day, goes out to lunch, and catches a movie.

PLANNED ISLAND HOPPING

Fun and games at the office are all good and fine. But why not lay the groundwork for some regular hard-core Island Hopping? For example, in the fitness arena, you might consider training for that Big Race even if you haven't decided to enter. We all know that guy in marketing who noisily announces he's training for the New York City Marathon, and uses that story to take off afternoons and enjoy two-hour lunches (for the entire yearlong buildup) because it eats up huge chunks of your day to run fifteen or twenty miles. The marathon card isn't for everyone. If you lack the right physique for anyone to remotely believe that you could possibly limp through 26.2 miles, consider a more plausible alternative: the 10K. Unless you're known to chain-smoke, you should be able to pull this off. Buy the props. The workout bag, the shoes, the sweats – maybe even wear the gear on Casual Friday. Announce you've got a training partner. You've got those can't-miss Tuesday/Thursday runs in Central Park at 5:30 p.m. that make it possible to skip all manner of awful meetings.

We can learn a lot about Island Hopping from naturals like Theresa, whom we met earlier: after earning her MBA at Stanford, she worked in brand management at Clorox. Theresa sailed off to one of her first Islands at Clorox when she announced she was going to train for her first half marathon. Breaking free of the office was easier than she imagined. "My manager was great," she says, adding that he signed on to her training schedule – "I could only stay till a certain time three days a week." Theresa had an easier time of it than most. She had already proved her ability to get her work done and be on the street by 6:00 p.m. – training regimen or not.

Of course, an athletic contest is only one planned Island Hopping getaway. Perhaps you're more the artsy type and can more easily sell your newfound passion for painting, sculpture, or ceramics. Some of these ideas may be more acceptable to superiors than others. Say you work with physical prototypes for new products. Who knows? Your bosses may see some logic in your shaping clay into unusual designs. But don't let practical considerations rule your passions. This is art. Maybe you just like sketching nudes. Or maybe you just like getting your hands muddy a couple of times a week. Or sketching nudes. Or fashioning weird structures out of found junk. Or sketching nudes. Or just not showing up for work on Fridays. "A lot of my teammates didn't say anything when I worked from home on Fridays," says Theresa of her time at Clorox. No surprise, then, that when Theresa first got out of business school and worked as a management consultant, she took a lot more than just Fridays off. "I took a leave of absence. I took three months off every summer because I wanted to learn Mandarin." It was years before she'd put in a full twelve months without taking off the summer. In response to her extended breaks, the consulting firm instituted a program to formalize leaves of absence. Theresa thinks people rarely explore all their options. "They don't create the opportunities. They say no to themselves or assume they're going to hear no."

The most straightforward course to getting the breaks you deserve – and need – is scheduled Island Hopping.

These are planned events that help you slice off the edges of your day. Maybe you only get out of work a half hour early, but it's amazing how many people thrive when they get even just thirty minutes to themselves.

Here's a sampling of Islands that people hop to:

▶ A Wall Street executive brings his lunch back to his desk and times himself solving the *New York Times* crossword puzzle. Every day. He says it tunes his mind for the pressure of the afternoon.

▶ Shelly, an architect for a major firm, leaves work early once a week to throw pots in her ceramics class.

▶ Tom, the CFO for a major university, leaves the office early once a week for his flute lesson.

▶ David, a financial trader at a San Francisco firm, rides his bike over the Golden Gate Bridge before dawn, arriving at work alert and energized. He says the return ride is the perfect cure for a crappy day.

▶ The head of a startup schedules several random meetings with some "professor of philosophy" or "wacky guy" every week. "My colleagues make this mistake of too often staying within the consensus of their industry group," he says. "You want someone dramatically outside to get fresh points of view."

▶ Elizabeth, a public-relations manager, practices her figure-skating routine from 6:30 to 7:30 a.m. four or five mornings a week and is in her cube with a view by 8:00 a.m. Elizabeth competed in the 2008 U.S. Adult Championships in Lake Placid, New York.

▶ Sharon, a quantitative analyst at a San Francisco energy firm, walks with a coworker across town and up the steep steps to the historic Coit Tower for a stunning bay view and terrific exercise – all on her lunch hour.

► A *Fortune* 500 VP spends several weekend days a month at the barn helping his daughter, who competes in equestrian events. "While she is getting ready, I get the tack. Then I pick out the hooves and bring the horse around. We curry [brush] it together and then she wraps the legs with polos [the horse equivalent of Ace bandages]. I put the saddle on. She rides while I watch. When she is done, I clean tack while she cleans the horse. We get done faster by dividing and conquering. The slow, careful pace of preparing for jumping is a great discipline and leadership-building experience." As a father, he finds it that rare parent-child reversal: "She is the expert."

► Eric, a hedge-fund manager, works out at his gym from a little after 4:00 until 5:00 every day – that's in the a.m. It sets him up for the whole day.

Your Island Hopping can be as directly or indirectly related to your "day job" as you want.

► Expected: The art director for an advertising firm begins painting landscapes.
► Unexpected: Studies French.
► Expected: The software engineer takes a computer-game design class.
► Unexpected: Joins an improv-comedy workshop.
► Expected: The human-resources director for a biomedical company takes a college course in human relations.
► Unexpected: Rows in a four before work twice a week.

UNDERWATER THINKING

Tom Zimmerman may work at IBM's Almaden Research Center in California by day, but in the past year, he's found his biggest ideas come outside of the office – literally underwater. A year ago, while learning to scuba dive, the fifty-year-old discovered that with the aid of a snorkel, he could suddenly swim for long stretches without bothering to come up for air. Zimmerman began visiting a local YMCA pool in the evenings and soon could swim for an hour underwater. It's become the perfect place to explore some of his most successful ideas for IBM. "When I'm underwater, it's almost like an isolation tank. There are no phones, no people," says Zimmerman. "I come in with an idea of what I want to work on. It's great for working out the big-picture stuff." His most ambitious watery exploration has grown into an IBM project to develop computer circuits that may eventually simulate the human brain. The swimming seems to supercharge his thinking. "My body keeps on swimming while my brain keeps working. I'm used to constructing things in my head before I build. I use my brain as a sketch board."

But Zimmerman also explores less lofty projects in the pool, like straightforward planning and management. He often scribbles down notes once he dries off or gets to his computer. His most successful underwater explorations are between 7:30 and 9:30 p.m., when the pool is relatively free of fish. "I can't make it work in the morning," he says. "It's like the rush hour. Too many people. You're always worried about crashing into somebody."

He's too nice to say it but we will. People get in the way of the ideas.

The key to Island Hopping is to get away – mentally and physically. Sailing may be one of the most liberating forms of Island Hopping. The lure of fresh salt air and open sea has torn many an adventurer from hearth and home. The difference today is that many of us have jobs and companies that don't permit us to pull up anchor and catch the wind. Dorian Banks, whom we met during our Switchblade chat, is proof that serious Island Hopping is possible for even the most plugged-in modern man. Banks owns several companies, teaches at Harvard, and mentors entrepreneurs. He is a two-BlackBerry man – as wired as they come. Proud of having laid down his share of 120-hour weeks. Few workdays end before 8:00 p.m., not to mention the cell calls and e-mails that pound in after the end of the formal day. But the Canadian Banks believes in the work-hard, play-hard life. Even on those demanding days, he gets in a walk with his dog and heads out for "beers and food" with friends.

But Tuesday-night racing is what really keeps him in tune. That time is sacrosanct. He cuts out of work at 4:00 p.m. to drive to the Vancouver harbor to climb onboard a thirty-five-footer and shove off. Banks loves getting some sun and air, but it's more than that. These are serious sailors – a breed apart. "They are not IT people. They're not entrepreneurs. They're not that motivated in work," says Banks. "They're sailors. If they had their choice, they wouldn't work at all."

Why hang with slackers every Tuesday?

Banks says that his father was a workaholic, and while he, too, loves his frenetic lifestyle, his weekly voyages somehow keep him from spinning out of control. "Sailing is such an insane diversion from business," he says. "A lot of things are similar, though. If the wind is stalling, you've got to make a decision. Do something different. Tack, open up new options. There are so many team analogies."

Banks races from 5:00 until 6:30 p.m., and then he and his mates just follow the wind, toss back a few beers as Canadians will do, and take in the sunset before heading back to the dock by 9:00 or 10:00 on those gloriously long Vancouver days.

Not a bad way to end a business day and be fresh for the morning.

ISLAND JAMMING

Some Island Hopping takes place in locations that aren't really places. Every Monday night at 7:30, a manager at a *Fortune* 100 company joins what he calls his "Leonardo group." He grabs his guitar, drives to a recording studio, and meets a drummer friend. "We plug in, turn on, and tune in," says the manager. He uses an application called Audacity to lay down multiple improvised tracks of music. "We make up songs, lyrics, chords, and melodies on the fly. We just improvise. It clears the palate." He plays guitar for the first two hours, piano for another. He says the weekly sessions zap his emotional RAM: difficult interpersonal run-ins and emotional duffel bags. Why at the launch of the workweek? It helps ground him in a creative way for the inevitable cascade of work nonsense ahead.

He's not alone. Renaissance men and women for centuries have realized the value of musical escape. You can look across the country and grab people from the loading dock up to the head office who get their release from corporate mind lock in the strings and sticks of the music studio. Consider finding the tunes that set you free.

Island Hopping Travel Tips

Here are four basic tips for successful corporate Island Hopping:

- ► **Stay Connected**
  If you're going to be Hopping for more than twenty minutes, be sure to check in with the office to see if you've had any calls that need to be returned or to ask if anyone is looking for you. Yes, you might have to leave the movie early, but hey, you only paid matinee prices.
- ► **Bring Back Treats**
  It never hurts to bring back surprise coffees or research materials for coworkers: "Jerry, here's a magazine I picked up for you that I thought would be great for that project you're working on!"
- ► **A Friend on the Inside**
  Keep your cell on and arrange for a trusted associate to call you if some kind of emergency in the office crops up.
- ► **Place Your Shots**
  Pull off your longer Hops when particularly noxious Spreadsheets and others who might object are out of the office themselves. Out of town is even better.

Island Hopping is how we maintain our sense of Soloist autonomy, creating both short and long stretches of time when we can pause, breathe, think . . . or just let everything shut down for a while. Become your own travel agent and start letting yourself get inspired about fun jaunts. Check out that hot new restaurant everyone's talking about. (Even if it's above your pay grade, grab an iced tea and hang out in the bar.) Pick up a travel magazine, and you'll be surprised at how much there is to do right around where you live that you didn't even know about. And if you know another Soloist at work who's stuck for Island Hopping ideas, don't be afraid to share yours — just don't give away your best secret getaway spots.

Bon voyage!

Time to Go Solo

If you really want to prove how serious you are about your career, it's time to take the critical step of recognizing the largest obstacle in your path.

People.

Start by asserting your need to be a Soloist. Make the *I Hate People!* discipline a key part of your business day, and you'll soon learn how to glide past the people who pose the biggest blockades in your way.

Now you've got a guide to help you recognize the Ten Least Wanted. You can anticipate the archetypes that cause you the most grief and aggravation: Switchblades, Bulldozers, Minute Men, and all the rest. You're smarter. You've reduced your exposure to the most toxic offenders. When contact is unavoidable, you'll emerge relatively unscathed. You're too wise to fall for the fantasy that everything will turn out fine if you're just nice. You've discovered that the team is not your salvation. No corporate groupthink will come to your rescue. If anything, *you* may be the answer to your company's ongoing challenge to break through to a new way of doing things.

As you take the lead as a Soloist, others will see you Solocrafting your way through the day.

Go ahead and dig your Cave. Trick out your cube or office to reflect your passions. And let those passions lead you to create the kind of breaks that will do you the most good: go Island Hopping in ways that will best grease the gears and spark the engine of productivity. Along the way, you'll find the subtle changes of pace that turn a people-clogged day into one that leaves you free to get everything done.

No longer is your day broken down into hours and minutes but, instead, people and more people. As you approach your daily tasks and chase your goals, you're acutely aware of the human factor: the men and women who are likely to stand in your way.

The time has come to bring all your newfound skills together. Like learning any new discipline – a sport or martial art – the key is rigorous, step-by-step training. Your training may begin right at your cube or office. Or you may take a more gradual approach, beginning with some "offline" efforts in social or community situations. Or you may decide to hell with the gradual, safe, and expected approach. Get down to some serious People Hating. In your office. Around your cube. In the bull pen. There's no time like today. Kick ass! Blow through a Stop Sign. Tear a Spreadsheet a new column. Shear some Sheeple. Enjoy yourself. As you chalk up more and more successful People Hating experiences, revel in the knowledge that this is important work. You're advancing your career and your company's prospects. Following in the footsteps of history's most brilliant Soloists.

This is serious stuff. The sort of stuff that can make a bad job bearable and a good job great. Just don't take it too seriously. And on those days when you're jammed for time and everyone's in your face, take a big deep breath, smile, and remind yourself:

"I hate people!"

Acknowledgments

We've come to the part of the book where we're supposed to acknowledge those who helped to make *I Hate People!* a reality. And it's time to come clean. There are some people that we don't hate.

This book nearly didn't happen. There were some in the world of publishing who thought you couldn't have the word *hate* in the title. Fretting that we might not get to write our book, we confess to having had a momentary lapse of strength. Yes, we nearly succumbed to the advice of soulless do-gooders who told us to scrub the H-word from the title.

But fortunately we were bolstered by a larger contingent that believed in our cause: Junie Dahn, our outstanding editor at Little, Brown, who had the wisdom to have us bring the hate. Heather Rizzo, Little Brown's director of publicity, who cottoned to our idea when it was just a few pages of paper, and proudly drank out of one our "I Hate People" coffee cups. Our agents, Jud Laghi and Kristine

Dahl, encouraged us to go forth and hate when others might have tried to rein us in with fear.

Diligent copyeditors Peggy Freudenthal and Nell Beram helped to make sure we didn't come off looking like big Know-It-Nones. And we'd like to send a big special bouquet of non-hate to our graphics guru, Bill Murray, for creating our fantastic cast of icons that helped put a face on some of our concepts and the Ten Least Wanted.

Yes, there were many we phoned or e-mailed for interviews who couldn't run fast enough from the idea of being associated with The Hate. But during this past year, we were also pleasantly surprised by the powerful response to our concept. Hundreds did talk to us or exchange e-mails: executives, managers, engineers, and entrepreneurs, who know in the pit of their stomachs that an honest approach to work begins with an acknowledgment of the people in the workplace. To these brave souls, we tip our hats. They are men and women who see the promise in playing the Soloist and breaking free of the chains of sugary niceness that have so clouded the corporate sphere.

These are the people who chuckled at our book title, regaled us with stories, and told us the secrets of how they find liberation and success against all odds. In them we see hope, a generation that understands that the key to success – in your career, family, and, dare we say, life – is a simple guiding force that keeps you on track:

"I Hate People!"

About the Authors

Jonathan Littman is the author of numerous acclaimed works of nonfiction, including *The Fugitive Game, The Watchman,* and *The Beautiful Game.* He is also the coauthor of IDEO's *The Art of Innovation* and *The Ten Faces of Innovation.* He is a contributing editor for *Playboy* and a columnist for Yahoo! Sports.

Marc Hershon is a branding expert who helped to create the names for the BlackBerry, Swiffer, nüvi, and many other influential products. He is also a comedy veteran who has worked closely with Dana Carvey, Bill Maher, and Robin Williams.

Visit www.IHatePeople.biz.